praise for STEAL THE SHOW

"If anyone knows how to steal the show, it's Michael Port. In this tour de force, he shares his secret method ~~on~~ ... rienced, can wow an audience."

— **Jeff Goins,** ...

"It takes decades of coaching and ... speaker. But it turns out, there's a s... ...ply Michael Port's principles to immediately stand out and steal the show."

— **Sally Hogshead, Hall of Fame Speaker and**
New York Times **best-selling author of** *How the World Sees You*

"An engaging book on how to dazzle audiences. Michael Port shares effective techniques for rehearsing and performing."

— **Adam Grant, Wharton professor and**
New York Times **best-selling author of** *Give and Take*

"Speaking in public is not just an art, it's a craft that can be learned and improved upon in order to discover treasures that can be mined. On that account, Port's latest book steals the show."

— **Peter Guber, CEO, Mandalay Entertainment, and**
#1 *New York Times* **best-selling author of** *Tell to Win*

"If you want to be effective in person — have people buy what you're selling, say 'yes' to your next big idea, follow your leadership, and, of course, give a killer speech — *Steal the Show* is the book for you."

— **Gabriel Weinberg, founder, DuckDuckGo.com and angel investor**

"From coaching NBA players to negotiating deals as the general manager to performing in media interviews and giving hundreds of keynote speeches, every aspect of my career has been about knowing how to influence individuals and audiences alike. *Steal the Show* delivers both important and useful lessons about how to consistently succeed in high-stakes situations. If you want to lead others, win negotiations, and be well liked, this book is for you." — **Carroll Dawson, former assistant coach**
and general manager of the Houston Rockets

STEAL THE SHOW

STEAL the SHOW

From Speeches to Job Interviews to Deal-Closing Pitches

*How to Guarantee a Standing Ovation for
All the Performances in Your Life*

Michael Port

HARPER

An Imprint of HarperCollins*Publishers*

Boston   New York

www.harpercollins.com

Library of Congress Cataloging-in-Publication Data
Port, Michael, date.
Steal the show : from speeches to job interviews to deal-closing
pitches, how to guarantee a standing ovation for all the
performances in your life / Michael Port.
pages cm
ISBN 978-0-544-55518-1 (hardback) — ISBN 978-0-544-55519-8 (ebook) —
ISBN 978-0-544-80084-7 (pbk.)
1. Business presentations. 2. Business communication. 3. Employment
interviewing. 4. Interpersonal communication. I. Title.
HF5718.22.P67 2015
658.4'52 — dc23
2015017313

Book design by Greta D. Sibley

Printed in the United States of America
23 24 25 26 27 LBC 16 15 14 13 12

for AMY

All the world's a stage,
And all the men and women merely players;
They have their exits and their entrances,
And one man in his time plays many parts . . .

— *William Shakespeare,* As You Like It

Contents

THE PERFORMER'S MINDSET

part 2

POWERFUL
PERFORMANCE PRINCIPLES

part 3
A MASTER CLASS IN PUBLIC SPEAKING

Author's Note

All the World's a Stage

YOU MAY HAVE PICKED UP THIS BOOK for many reasons. Perhaps you have a speech to deliver at an industry conference. Maybe you're attempting to land a big project. You could be preparing for a job interview that will make or break your career. Maybe you're cramming for a meeting you'll be leading with senior staff in attendance eyeballing your performance. It's possible you want to pitch a new business idea and you have to present it to a group of venture capitalists or bank executives. While these are distinct experiences they share a common thread: they all require you to *perform*.

Which is really scary. No matter how clever you are or how good you are at what you do, the performance side of these events can be anxiety provoking and intimidating.

And, when I say *perform,* I don't just mean that you will do something or complete something. I mean that you will present, act, stage, show, or dramatize; put on a performance that delights, impresses, wows, connects, or moves people to think, feel, or do something different.

You may think that only actors perform — onstage or in the movies — but the reality is, we are all performers. Think about it. When you Skype for a conference call or speak on a panel, you're performing. When you use social media or describe yourself on a dating site, you're presenting yourself in a particular way and are therefore performing. When you express yourself in meetings, pitch a client, or walk into a job interview, you're performing. Even when you're trying to play it cool and keep a low profile, you're performing. (C'mon, admit it — that time you were at your boss's holiday party and you were sipping your drink casually by the pool with a look of quiet thoughtfulness, you were performing too.) Whether we want to admit it or not, our professional lives are full of public moments we can't escape and can't afford to screw up. In our personal lives, we're often called upon to deliver toasts, eulogies, graduation remarks, or inspirational talks before a civic group — even a first date is a kind of performance.

The irony is, most of us have to perform, even though we don't see ourselves as performers.

Yet, I can almost hear you saying, "Well, I'm not really a performer and I'm certainly not an actor; in fact, I'm far from it. Actors love the spotlight and can't wait to get onstage. I'm shy and I get visibly nervous when I have to speak in front of others."

Well, I have good news for you. That's fantastic. No, it's better than that. It's a "you-just-won-the-lottery" kind of fantastic. You're exactly the person for whom I've written this book.

In *Steal the Show,* you'll discover the role you want to play in the show that is your own life. You'll decide whether you are up for a leading or supporting role. Often we make the choice to play small because we haven't given ourselves the chance to see the big opportunities in front of us. Not everyone is going to be a comedian or even a natural-born entertainer. But you don't need to be an *entertainer* to be a *performer.* Performance can be about wowing an audience, but it can also simply be about connecting with others, which is a beautiful thing.

Through this book you will learn how to leverage performance skills along with what you know — your backstory, beliefs, expertise, and values — to find the authenticity in the roles you choose to play. Finding this authenticity and then having the courage to use it is how you become an effective communicator and leader — no matter how nervous you may feel reading this today.

As a writer, professional speaker, and owner of multiple businesses, I am often scared myself, but I have also learned that it's what we do with that fear that makes us who we are. In this book, I reveal how I was only able to meet the goals I'd set for myself by fully embracing my fears and drawing upon what my classical training as an actor at NYU's Graduate Acting Program taught me about the power of great performances.

You see, my first career was as an actor. This was well before I was a business owner and wrote five business books, including *Book Yourself Solid, Book Yourself Solid Illustrated, Beyond Booked Solid, The Contrarian Effect,* and *The Think Big Manifesto.* Maybe you saw me on some of your favorite TV programs in the '90s, including *Sex & the City, Third Watch, All My Children,* and *Law and Order,* among others — only then with a full head of hair.

I'm buzzing with anticipation to share with you the most amazing way that the dramatic concepts of acting, stagecraft, and improvisation can help you communicate, speak, make deals, build and run a business, market your products, and try new things. I'm living proof that an actor's knowledge can be translated into everyday tactics that anyone can adopt and use for professional success.

In fact, when I retired from the ranks of professional actors, I nailed my first corporate job interview (for which I was completely unqualified). I landed "the part" because of my ability to authentically "play the role" required. I pulled it off by in effect saying, "I know on paper I'm not qualified for this position, but here's why I think you should hire me." I was able to do this because of the principles and techniques I had mastered as an actor.

I have spent the better part of this decade creating a modern methodology that can help you become a better performer. Through this book, I will teach you everyday performance principles and techniques that I've designed specifically for nonactors so you can overcome your fears; silence your critics, both internal and external; find your voice; and become a confident performer in the spotlight.

Acting is not a metaphor but rather a model that you can apply to both life and work.

Why do I say this? Because, to paraphrase the legendary acting teacher Lee Strasberg, an actor's work is about the ability to consistently create reality and to express that reality. And that is in large part the way that life works for all of us. Each day we have the ability to create our reality. I don't mean this as an abundance theory, that we're using affirmations or writing poetry (neither of which I do but both of which are perfectly good things to do), but rather that all of us inevitably make choices about what we want to achieve every day and over the course of years and decades. Those choices form a narrative, a narrative that tells the story of our lives. In parallel, we have choices about how we will express ourselves publicly to meet those aspirations. Performance, at its core, is about how you communicate and, by extension, how you connect with others on a daily basis. The truth behind why some performers captivate an audience while others lull an audience into checking their phones is found in the creative history and unique craft of acting, which can be used as a model for successful performance in both personal and professional life.

We may not have had the pleasure of meeting, but through the pages of this book we'll be spending time together. I know that many people compete for your attention and that you have many demands on your time. I feel blessed and grateful to have the opportunity to be of service to you, and I never take that honor for granted. I'm here for you, as are my partners and team. If you or your organization ever needs help, please don't hesitate to contact us at questions@michaelport.com, or visit StealTheShow.com for more information, including free tips and video training lessons on public speaking. And, most importantly, as you read through the pages of this book, please remember to think *big* about who you are and what you offer the world.

Warmly,

Michael Port

Prologue

Make the Most of the Spotlight Moments in Your Life

FOR OUR WORK TOGETHER, please note the following:

1. *Steal the Show* is about how you can use insights from the craft of acting to improve all the performances in your life: give better speeches, nail interviews, close deals, have effective conversations, lead teams, and, as crazy as it might seem, have even more love and romance in your life. *Steal the Show* is not about acting and is not *for* actors. It's for *you*, the non-actor. Moreover, there's nothing inherently special about actors as compared to people in any other profession. Rather, it's what you learn from *acting* (as applied to all the performances in your life) that's of great value.

2. Throughout the book, when I say *audience* I'm referring to anyone who is party to or part of your performance in any way: an interviewer, a supervisor, your staff, a client, a romantic interest, a project team, wedding guests, students,

the members of your local Chamber of Commerce, and, of course, a theater full of attendees at a convention.

3. In the theater, the concept of "stealing the show" is a gift to the audience and your fellow performers. Sure, the performer who steals the show gets a standing ovation and benefits from the personal accolades her performance has brought about — but there is no greater gift to the audience than for someone to steal the show. The audience *wants* to be blown away by a performance. And the same applies in settings other than theater. Don't confuse stealing the show with upstaging other performers, which is a big no-no. Stealing the show is ultimately about how you can make any performance better for your audience (remember my definition of *audience* from above).

Acting at its best is, in fact, grounded in *reality*. By learning from it, you'll be more confident and comfortable (and less terrified) every time you're expected to carry the moment as a speaker, presenter, leader, or player in any of life's most important moments.

Through this book you will learn how to understand and act upon insights, including how to:

- Overcome stage fright and become comfortable in your own body, and then how to live in the moment during public presentations, from one-on-one meetings to sales calls to keynote talks;

- Take smart risks and raise the stakes in business and personal situations;

- Master the elements of writing and storytelling so you can change minds and lives;

- Use the underappreciated power of acting "as if . . ." to find your voice and confidence in new or nerve-wracking networking and speaking situations;

- Understand the technique of saying *yes, and . . .* , which leads to better meetings, conference calls, team performances, and presentations;

- Imagine and step into new roles personally and professionally without feeling phony;

- Draw on the power of performance to influence others and silence the critics;

- Master the elements of effective rehearsal for all situations where you need to impress and move people to think, feel, or act differently;

- Use the secrets of improvisation so when things go wrong, you can actually turn those moments into the best moments of your show and perhaps your life.

But that's only the beginning. The techniques and principles I'll teach you apply to the demands of just about any profession; consulting, professional services, management, marketing, small business and entrepreneurship, computing, teaching, nonprofit leadership — you name it. These techniques and principles also help in life's many unpredictable moments, such as stepping in for the boss at a big meeting, attending a new professional meet-up when you're tired and out of sorts, or delivering an improvised speech at a nephew's graduation party.

EXPRESS YOURSELF WITH
CLEAR INTENT AND PURPOSE

What I share with you in *Steal the Show* will also help you be honest and true to yourself and your abilities and not act in ways that can be seen as phony or self-promoting. The best performers in the world are the most honest ones. Many of the world's best performers are quiet, dedicated, sensitive artists who reserve their energy for their work in service of an audience. In fact, the most important elements of preparing for a great performance have less to do with self-expression and more to do with self-understanding. *Self-expression* is often simply used as a means of emoting or sharing how you feel. *Self-understanding* allows you to express yourself with clear intent and purpose that resonates with the people around you.

The rub is that being honest, emotionally available, vulnerable, and transparent in front of others can be terrifying. To combat stage fright, people have been told that they should picture the audience in their underwear. That's some of the worst (and weirdest) advice ever given, for two reasons: First, if you think about your audience in their underwear or, worse yet, naked, then it's going to be really difficult to focus on your presentation. Second, seeing the people all around you in their full glory may, in reality, actually make you even more nervous. The truth is . . . it's the performer who's naked — metaphorically speaking, of course. As the great actress Rosalind Russell once observed: "Acting is standing up naked and turning around very slowly."

Being worried about performing in public affects almost everybody. If you're nervous about your next presentation or speech, well, that's only natural. If the butterflies are propagating and swarming and making your stomach stew and your heartbeat hammer, that's to be expected. But once you learn how to live with these fears, you will show the people on your team and many others the way forward.

Performing and communicating are always about building up, not tearing down. You can be a critic *or* a performer, I believe, but you can't be both. Anyone can tear something down; the trick is to build something better in its place. As a performer and an active player in my own life and work, I have little interest in critics. Great performances require taking risks. To take those risks not only do you need to silence the external critics, you also need to let go of the inner critic that tries to worry you about the fear of rejection.

FIND YOUR VOICE

Great performances are developed and won from the inside out. You won't communicate and speak successfully just by learning body language, stage tricks, and elocution tips. The benefits will fade and you'll revert to old habits that those who get sucked into quick-fix diets know well; a loss of a few pounds is followed by the quick gain of a few more. The simplest way to overcome stage fright or performance anxiety is to actually know what you're doing when you're on the stage or in a high-pressure situation. Joni Zander discovered this firsthand during one of the most important moments of her life: "My training in Michael Port's Heroic Public Speaking program came in handy this weekend. I was able to say my wedding vows clearly, confidently, and expressively. Before, I would have cried through the whole thing and not been able to get the words out. Public speaking skills are so important and I'm happy to have had the best training." When you're finished with this book, you will, without a doubt, know not only how to handle yourself but also how to make the most of the spotlight moments of your life in meetings, interviews, sales presentations, wedding toasts, on big stages, and in dozens of other situations that call on you to carry the day.

If performing were easy, you wouldn't find 90 million Google results when you search for "public speaking." Articles, videos, and books about communications, speaking, and persuasion are as common as actors in LA. But learning to become an effective speaker and performer isn't like taking a Xanax to manage your anxiety for a day or two. You need more than just a typical laundry list of sophomoric bullet-point tips: know your material, relax, visualize yourself being fabulous, use your hands, make eye contact, gain experience. Rather, it's about realizing a huge, underserved, and unexplored area of your creative potential in order to become far more successful both professionally and personally. As a participant at one of my public-speaking training events shared: "I thought I was coming to learn techniques to be a better communicator and speaker but I was astonished to find that you were able to help me — and every person in the room — find their voice, increase their confidence, be authentic, and think big. I thought that maybe acting or performing was about being phony or staged but what I discovered is that performing is about being more honest and more real. I am, for the better, forever changed. I am grateful."

Maybe you avoid being center stage or in high-stakes situations so you hold yourself back from getting promoted or taking on a new sales territory or going after more sales meetings. Or maybe you think you're clever and charming and have been getting away with winging it for far too long. Maybe you're coasting on the laurels of past performances but not staying up to date with technology, with what audiences expect, and most of all, the expansiveness of your own talent. Or maybe you're dreaming of sharing your message with thousands of people but just don't yet know how to perform with skill, style, grace, and impact. Perhaps you're just tired of sitting in the cheap seats of life watching others steal the show.

Whether you lack confidence or experience, or you do have experience but found you've hit a wall in your approach and want to discover how you can get even better, my answer is yes, you *can* steal the show.

HOW MY METHOD WORKS

Now that I've shared the premise of the book and why the techniques actors use are so essential to work-related and other performances, let's discuss where we're going and how this is all going to work. *Steal the Show* is divided into three parts that are made up of different chapters.

Part I: The Performer's Mindset

In Part I, you'll learn the keys to the performer's mindset. You'll begin by finding your voice and the strength to use it. You'll discover how to play the right role in any situation and learn that you can authentically (there's that word again) play many different roles in many different scenarios. Of course, first you need to identify the various roles you already play, along with which ones you want to keep playing and which ones you want to retire. Then you will once and for all crush your fears and silence the critics ... you know, the ones front and center inside your head as well as those in the cheap seats who invariably find fault with others. Through this process, the Performer's Mindset will prepare you, psychologically and emotionally, to perform in ways that overcome objections and stir the heart.

Chapter 1: Find Your Voice

This is the first step to mastering the inner game of standing out. You'll finally embrace and choose to own your specific and unique strengths as a performer. This is where you dispel the doubts about the roles you want to play and the dreams you want to live. You'll examine your self-image and prejudices about performing, inventory your mental filters, and scrape away your false personae.

Chapter 2: Play the Right Role in Every Situation

You may see yourself as one kind of performer but have the potential to be another. By amplifying the most compelling parts of your personality, you will inspire and motivate others. You'll feel comfortable in almost any situation.

Chapter 3: Crush Your Fears and Silence the Critics

Learning how to deal with criticism and negativity is required if you want to perform. I'll show you how to silence the critics, both your own internal voices of doubt and fear as well as the external voices of those who inevitably find fault with your message. I'll help you see that it's part of your job to hear the criticism and to move on or sometimes simply ignore it altogether. It's also important to differentiate between toxic feedback and helpful objective support.

Part II: Powerful Performance Principles

The next part includes six short, punchy chapters. In each one, I share one of the six performance principles that will help you win the day every day. These principles enable entrepreneurs, athletes, managers, and others to steal the show in their presentations, meetings, sales pitches, negotiations, and more. Think of this part as the "operating system" for each stage of your next performance.

Chapter 4: Have a Clear Objective

This is the foundation. Your first step activates a clear vision of what you want to accomplish — your "why you do it." That is, establish where you want to go, what you want to accomplish, and why.

Chapter 5: Act "As if . . ."

This is an imagination-expanding technique that helps you overcome worrisome behaviors and fears so you can begin to make *intentional* choices about how you want to perform and what you
want to achieve — even if you don't yet believe you can.

Chapter 6: Raise the Stakes

Discover how to evaluate and take smart risks to overcome your
anxiety about stepping up and standing out. The truth is, no one
ever succeeded by playing small. Do you want to set a new sales record for yourself? Then go out of your way to meet more people. Do
you want to get booked to speak at the largest industry conference?
Be willing to be provocative and boldly share your message in the
face of potential criticism. We're wired to stick with what's familiar and view risk as something to avoid at all costs. But keep in mind
that the good decisions you've already made in your life all carried
some risk — from asking out your future partner to interviewing for
a job in a new field. What's more, the risk of inaction is stagnation
whereas the reward of action is traction.

Chapter 7: Say "Yes, and . . ."

Even in difficult conversations, or situations that you'd normally
back away from because they're overwhelming or seem just too
challenging, you can be part of the solution by understanding and
using the simple phrase *yes, and . . .*

Chapter 8: Be in the Moment

This skill empowers you to respond to the changing realities and
unexpected developments of the moment (while nonetheless being

fully rehearsed) with choices that are authentic, fresh, and consistent. It's the foundation for improvisation – not just onstage but also on sales calls, or even dates. Oh, and they come in handy when you need to think on your feet when negotiating the purchase of a new car or boat. (You can't buy happiness, but you can buy a boat, and for me, that's pretty much the same thing.)

Chapter 9: Choose Early and Often

Get to where you want to go quickly. If what you're doing works, carry on. If it doesn't, scrap it and make a better choice. This is different than being fickle, flaky, or faithless. People who make strong choices are compelling, confident, and commanding. I don't want to work with someone who perseverates or procrastinates and sits on his hands waiting for something to miraculously happen or for someone to tell him what to do. Do you?

Part III: A Master Class in Public Speaking

This part draws on the mental work of Part I as well as the principles you learned in Part II to teach you the technical and practical aspects of performing and public speaking – so you can take center stage, own the room, and give show-stealing performances.

Chapter 10: How to Craft Captivating Pitches, Speeches, and Stories

Whether you are a spreadsheet wizard who is put off by having to write a birthday card, a professional author looking for a few tips, or, more likely, someone in between these extremes, this chapter provides a nearly never-fail, faithful companion to content creation that will empower you to craft speeches, responses to interview questions, pitches, and performances.

Chapter 11: How to Create and
Tell Stories That Make 'Em Laugh or Cry

Most of us would like to have the ability to develop and tell a well-crafted story and effortlessly deliver a joke that people love in any setting. In this chapter, you'll learn how to get there in a way that is authentic to you and your personality. You may be intimidated by telling stories or jokes but I will demystify how they work and give you a simple process to create and present your own material.

Chapter 12: How to Rehearse and
Stage World-Class Performances

If you want to steal the show and create a meaningful experience for your audience, and if you want to truly own your career's spotlight moments, you probably need to prepare differently than you have in the past. This means rehearsing in a way that leaves little to chance for your big moment. I will guide you through a seven-step protocol for effective rehearsals that will keep your nerves at bay and help you achieve all the potential you have for a particular performance.

Chapter 13: How to Produce Powerful Openings,
Commanding Closings, and Amazing Audience Interaction

Get an invaluable storehouse of techniques and examples for openings, closings, and audience interactions, as well as creative finishing touches that are useful for any presentation. Everyone I've coached has seen significant benefits from these strategies over time. They also become a lot of fun to use, and they instill confidence by anchoring your presentation as one that you know will start and finish strong.

Chapter 14: How to Improvise Your Way into the Hearts and Minds of the Toughest Crowds

Improvisation is one of the most powerful secrets from the world of acting. It is a creative, nonjudgmental, open-ended approach to unscripted scenarios and live possibilities. In this chapter I'll show you how it works, how to use it to perk up your performances, and how to apply its underlying capabilities to many business situations.

Chapter 15: How to Get a Standing Ovation Every Time—Really

It's time to put it all together and to master the big move to the performance itself, with tips and strategies for connecting at a psychological, practical, and emotional level with your audience through my five keys to a show-stealing performance. They are the pre-show ritual, developing stage awareness, owning the room, creating intimate moments, and managing the post-show cycle.

You may have skipped ahead and checked out Part III, where there is lots of instruction, specifically for giving speeches, that you can use right away. So why didn't I start the book from the outside in, with the techniques you'll be learning in Part III? Why did I start from the inside out, with the more challenging issues of fear, anxiety, role-playing, and finding your voice, and then move into the performance principles? It would be easy to start with how-to techniques that you can layer on top of your performances immediately. However, I made this choice because I'm asking you to change the way you do things when it comes to speaking and communicating. I'm asking you to see the world in a different way. I'm asking you to find a new way of being around performance. By switching your perspective this way you will:

- Discover more about your strengths as a public speaker;
- See how the foundations of the actor's craft can apply to you, the nonactor, in all performance situations in your life;
- Decide you're ready to play a bigger role in your own career and life.

As a result, the instructional material in Part III will be easier to absorb, learn, and make your own when you get there.

The personal and professional challenges we all face are multi-faceted and always changing. The truth is, you can be called on at any minute to appear in front of a client, boss, the entire office staff, or even onstage in front of hundreds of peers.

Yes, maybe you've survived so far by being a "good enough" performer because you think you're good at winging it. But you know as well as I do that the stakes and expectations are changing – at least they are if you're ambitious and have goals and dreams and you truly want to fulfill your potential.

All the choices you make in your life signal to people, *This is what I want you to know about me.*

I will teach you what the best actors, marketers, business managers, and entrepreneurs know: their success is empowered by public performance told through true stories they believe and characters they create. It's time for you to step out of the wings, onto the stage, and steal the show . . . no matter what you want to do with your life.

part **1**

THE PERFORMER'S MINDSET

We're going to start with the performer's mindset. This way, you'll be prepared, psychologically and emotionally, to perform in ways that stir the heart and inspire action. In order to do this, your desire to perform needs to be stronger than your fear of criticism or failure, your voice must be powerful and in tune with your values and beliefs, and you'll need to know how to play the right role in every situation. Once you've read through this first part of the book and adopted the performer's mindset, you'll see performance from a different, more empowering perspective and you'll be on your way to stealing the show during the most important high-stakes situations of your life.

1

Find Your Voice

THE MOST COMMON MISSING ELEMENT in the thousands of presentations and performances I've witnessed is the speaker's true voice. But finding your voice can be difficult for many people in business and life, even for those building careers as top executives, thought leaders, or performers.

Here's an illustration of why finding and *trusting* your voice matters even to advanced speakers. A client of mine appeared on a major broadcast network, and her program excelled in numerous ways. However, during the first segment, I noticed that she was apologizing for telling parts of her life story, along the lines of "I'm sorry for sharing about myself again," or, "I apologize for sharing this . . ." I chatted with her during the break and told her she was doing great. She asked if I had any notes for her. So I offered: "How would you feel about doing away with all of your apologies for sharing? You're on the stage to share. That's why you're there." Apologizing for sharing is a way of saying you're sorry for your own voice.

Research has shown that women tend to apologize more than men. Two studies by the University of Waterloo in Ontario and published in the journal *Psychological Science* in 2010 found that while men are just as willing as women to apologize, they have a higher threshold for what they feel they need to apologize for.

My client agreed to try dropping the unneeded apologies and we talked about how anyone, including the two of us, can get caught in the perfection trap, wondering if we're worthy of the moment. In public speaking or, say, during the interview process for a new job, it's easy to get distracted and start questioning yourself: What can I say that hasn't already been said? What can I do that hasn't already been done? Why should I be here rather than someone else? Finding your true voice can help you realize that none of those questions are as important as how you say what you say to put into perspective the personal journey that raised those doubts along the way.

So what is finding your true voice?

For starters, it's about letting go of your inner critic, the voices in your head telling you you're not good enough, don't know enough, and don't have enough. It's about saying *Goodbye, thanks for sharing,* to those inner voices carping that you might not be ready, qualified, or worthy of the next opportunity.

Letting go of thinking you don't have enough to offer is an incredibly rewarding aspect of what I am sharing in this book. It allows you to embrace your gifts so you have the confidence and natural conviction that you can get results from your performances and speeches. Even if you're saying something that's already been said, *it's your voice that matters.* You don't have to be different to make a difference. How many mothers sing the same lullabies to their children? A baby doesn't care half as much about the song as she does about the sound of her mother's voice.

Perhaps you are blessed with sturdy self-esteem, feel like you were born to stand in the spotlight, and don't second-guess your performances. If so, feel free to keep your Superman costume. I suppose it comes easy for a lucky few. (Of course, it might just be bravado; the way you tell the difference is by assessing whether or not you continually raise the stakes and allow yourself to be comfortable with discomfort.)

Finding your voice is important for your results. If you want to play different roles authentically and amplify or downplay different parts of your personality to do so, it's important to be comfortable with who you really are and what you stand for so you never lose sight of your values.

Too often, when you are given any opportunity to be in the spotlight, you get scared and lose the sense of being authentic and performing in the moment. Instead, you *play at* what you think a person in that situation is *supposed* to be like. As a result, you believe that you're an imposter. However, by learning how to be yourself when you perform, while also embracing the fact that you can be a chameleon who plays lots of different roles with different styles of behavior, you will become a powerful performer and speaker.

It might seem like a contradiction — be yourself but also be a chameleon. F. Scott Fitzgerald saw "the ability to hold two opposing ideas in mind at the same time and still retain the ability to function" as the sign of a well-developed intelligence. I suspect you have that ability. So, please, for the time being, just hold this idea in your head: that you can play different roles and still be authentic. The payoff will be the discovery of the abilities, strengths, and enthusiasm that you possess as a performer.

Some of us will, at times, add on layers of personae to gain others' approval while hiding parts of ourselves that we think are embarrassing. Authenticity really comes down to this question: do you have the courage to talk about who you really are, not just who you want others to think you are?

This is different than sharing inappropriate information or

unnecessary historical details. It's important to listen actively, to be curious about others, and to have a sense of proportion about how much you talk about yourself. We don't need to know the details of Sam's late-night rendezvous or how Susie feels like she isn't worthy of the promotion she received. The former is inappropriate and something that Sam should keep private. The latter is self-destructive and should be discussed only with trusted mentors and advisors in order to overcome it; Susie could lose credibility with her subordinates if she discusses it with them.

At the same time, many extraordinarily successful people learn how to "own" the key elements of their backstory and make them part of their public personality and statements. *In the right circumstances,* when you're open about your weaknesses, differences, or difficulties, people find you more approachable and they will connect at a deeper level with your message. We've seen in our own social history how accountability to personal truths propels a talented person to new levels. Robin Roberts's career at ABC gained new clarity and credibility when she opened up about being gay. Facebook COO Sheryl Sandberg's success as the author of the bestselling book *Lean In* and the movement it spurred was due to her ability to communicate her own conflicts around children, intimacy, and marriage to women from vastly different backgrounds. She was willing to share that she doesn't have it all figured out. It was Howard Shultz's openness about the destructiveness of his own overreaching ambition that kicked off the Starbucks reboot that took place in 2008.

THE FEAR OF BEING FOUND OUT

This first part of the book will help you master the inner game of performance. You want to improve as a performer and speaker. You're committing to being authentic to your personal biography and style. Perhaps you've identified areas for improvement, such as nervousness, a lack of imagination, boring content, stiffness, predictability, lack of humor; those issues are personal to you. Maybe you've identified childhood experiences that affected your self-image and self-esteem as a performer, such as the criticism of a parent or a sibling who was more of a natural performer and intimidated you. Perhaps you were an outsider in high school and internalized that sense of not belonging in the spotlight. Your supervisor or peers may have negatively critiqued a performance or presentation and it has stuck with you for years.

These stories are not uncommon. They're universal. They feed the anxiety about performing that is also universal. The biggest issue isn't nerves — that's normal. But these negative filters turn your perspective inward. When it comes to a high-stakes business performance, you might fear you'll be found out for not having what it takes, for being a fraud in a suit. Not "fraud" as in con man. But, rather, fraud, as in people will find out you're not the confident, expert leader you're pretending to be. Isn't that why it's such a big relief when a potential performance is canceled or postponed? *Whew! They won't find me out this time!* I don't want you to get stuck in the rut of performing so you're not found out. And I don't think you do either.

Steal the Show is about delivering big results for you and your career. It's not about getting approval or keeping your head down or doing just enough to stay in your job. You can't perform your way into universal job protection. Perform to win. Perform to achieve business goals by trusting your preparation and your true persona.

FREEING YOUR NATURAL VOICE

There are important behaviors that open the way to freeing your voice and finding a sense of self-esteem and self-possession as a performer. These include:

- Finding out what it takes to discover your backstory, and keeping your promises to your audience (whomever and wherever they may be).
- Letting go of the pernicious small thoughts that maintain the illusion that your voice shouldn't be heard.
- Escaping the perfection trap in embracing your role as a performer.
- Never again being trapped by your history or anyone else's.
- Embracing your audience with love.

I admire the pioneering work of teacher, author, and psychotherapist Dr. Nathaniel Branden. His definition of self-esteem is one that I aspire to as an individual and suggest that my students consider as well: "Self-esteem is the disposition to experience oneself as being competent to cope with the basic challenges of life, and as being worthy of happiness. Thus, it consists of two components: (1) self-efficacy — confidence in one's ability to think, learn, choose, and make appropriate decisions; and (2) self-respect — confidence that love, friendship, achievement, success — in a word, happiness — are natural and appropriate."[1]

KNOWING WHEN YOUR VOICE IS ALREADY THERE

A big advantage of the performing techniques and strategies in this book, and of rehearsing them properly, is that you will strengthen these two types of confidence, self-efficacy and self-respect, and starve the inner nags of the oxygen they need. This has worked for many of my students, including Lori, a CPA who attended one of my events in 2013.

Lori doesn't possess a big, charismatic performer's personality. Rather, she's a quiet, reserved number cruncher. Lori told me she was fearful of speaking in public and enrolled in the event because she needed to find her voice and have more confidence in meetings and at professional conferences. During the seminar, Lori found it hard to hold center stage with confidence or project her voice more than a few feet. I saw her hands shaking as she clutched her note cards. When I snuck up on her and took the cards away, Lori cursed me under her breath. I was both shocked and delighted by Lori's response. Most of all, however, I could hardly wait to see what she would do next.

Without her cards to hide behind, Lori addressed her fears of public speaking and challenges with making herself heard, for what might have been the first time. She shared that she'd been hiding most of her life. The one time she tried to speak up as a child, her mother slapped her across the face and said, "No one wants to hear from you." That one moment shut her up for over forty years. In a seminar that included professional speakers, she was the only student who brought the room to tears with her speech. Lori overcame her fears by investing herself in a method that freed her from her past and allowed her to find her own voice in the present.

The accomplished actress Jamie Lee Curtis found a whole new voice in writing and speaking about addiction and recovery: she claims her fifteen years of sobriety as her greatest achievement. Her blog *Good Morning Heartache, Good Morning Life* on *The Huffington Post* is regularly shared and retweeted by thousands. Former actress and mental health expert Kathy Cronkite (Walter's daughter) went public with her struggles living with severe depression, leaving her career as an actress to become a popular, influential advocate for mental health treatment. Now she is a popular keynote speaker.

You see, finding your voice isn't necessarily a matter of adding things. It's certainly not about becoming someone else. Maybe it's not a matter of *finding* it at all, but rather just the opposite. Maybe it's about stripping away the false personae and excesses since your voice is already there. It's about returning to who you were before you started believing other people's stories about you. It's you. It's your core.

DON'T TALK YOURSELF OUT OF SUCCESS

Don't let your voice be trapped by history. The past doesn't have to predict whether or not you will have success. So many people talk themselves out of their dreams because they've had letdowns in the past. That's a common pitfall. For example, Frederick Banting, who won the 1923 Nobel Prize in Medicine for his discovery of insulin's ability to control diabetes in humans, said in his later years that, if he had been more familiar with the literature and the long history of unsuccessful attempts to isolate the hormone, he might never have undertaken the research that was ultimately successful.

I feel similarly about writing books. If I have too many other voices or points of view in my head, I start questioning myself or I write in response to what others are saying. Neither of these situations is how I'd like to spend my time. And I certainly don't want to censor myself and not write about a concept that is central to my methodology because someone else has already addressed it. Of course, I read and pay attention to the world around me. I don't lock myself in a dark room and avoid the world in order to find my voice. But, when it comes time to create, I trust my voice. And you should too.

The problem with fixating on other people's histories of failed expectations is that it makes you think small and play small. The notion that being "realistic" or practical means settling for less is a small idea that robs you of your voice. It is realistic and practical for you to do big things. Eleanor Roosevelt said, "The future belongs to those who believe in the beauty of their dreams." For our work together, think of it like this: the future belongs to those who believe in the beauty of their dreams and have the willingness to find their voice and confidently and proudly share it with others.

PUNCTURING THE PERFECTION MYTH

Trusting your voice means that you rehearse and perform to achieve your goals, communicate a big idea, and get results. It doesn't mean you set out even subconsciously to "prove" you're better than other speakers, or to make the audience like you. By making your goals unrealistic and unattainable, you'll start playing small and diminishing your voice and presence. When you are in the spotlight, yes, many people are looking to you for answers. But that doesn't mean you must have all the answers. You just need to be able to deliver on your promise.

You don't have to be the smartest person in the room to present and deliver compelling content in a speech, effectively lead a brainstorming session, or even get chosen for a leadership position. Sometimes the way to increase your status in the eyes of others is to say, "I don't know." The one who thinks she always knows what's best is usually the last one to be asked for her opinion. As I mentioned earlier, what you say doesn't have to be different to make a difference. It's *the way* you say it that matters. Your particular voice connects with some people and not with others.

For example, if you sit on a conference panel, you might be drawn into competition over whether you will speak first, last, or in the middle of a program. Yes, often the first one to voice her opinion can set the tone. There are times when finding your voice after you hear what others have to say (in a meeting) is the most powerful choice; it resonates the strongest and reverberates the loudest. So, sometimes, the first one to take the stage is the last one remembered.

WHEN YOUR VOICE IS THE STRONGEST

As you advance into my methodology, consider this: *to be exposed when you are performing is where your true strength resides.* When you think you have to protect yourself from getting hurt, from the power of others to adversely affect your life, all you have really done is repress your dreams. You have wasted your voice on self-protection, rather than amplifying it through self-understanding followed by self-expression. All that negativity makes you weak. Your voice is strong when it is founded on generosity and, dare I say it, love.

In fact, I suggest trying to love every member of your audience even if they're thumbing their noses at you. When you're given the stage or any kind of platform, like the head of the table at Thanksgiving dinner, it's an honor. Call me corny but that's the way I see it. Later in the book, I'll discuss how to get the audience to respect you even before you stand in front of them. That's when your voice is the strongest.

Finding your voice and speaking up probably shouldn't be a rebellious act. It's empowerment, not revolt. It's not a response to something; it's not "I'm-going-to-show-them-just-watch-me . . ." To rebel is an action fueled by scarcity. It's a small voice shouting. Finding and sharing your voice is about creating something new, not simply complaining or rebelling against something in the past.

The exciting performer breaks the rules — not just to be rebellious but to create something new, something that works better than what currently exists, and to delight, surprise, enthrall, move, and inspire. The act of tearing something down without rebuilding something better in its place traps us in the past rather than freeing us to experience the rewards of the future.

Play the Right Role in Every Situation

I always am in a role, lovely — for you, for them — even for myself.
Yeah . . . Even when I'm alone, I am still in a role — and I
myself am the most exacting audience I have ever had.

— *Simona Panova, author of* Nightmarish Sacrifice

MANY OF THE WORLD'S GREATEST LEADERS, along with effective people from all walks of life, know how to play different yet still authentic roles that help them fit in with many diverse groups of people in scenarios of all kinds. Whether you're preparing for a presentation, being promoted, being reassigned to a new position, or finding that you have grown stagnant in your current life or business circumstances, discovering how to play different roles and to adopt new styles of behavior powers up your creativity and confidence.

Playing the right role is about identifying how you fit into a given scenario — and stealing the show when you do. This chapter will help you develop new skills to present, pitch, and perform based on your strengths and interests. It's about building on who you are, what you stand for, and what you already do — and doing it for a purpose. When you're playing the *right* roles, you are persuasive in those roles because they're *authentic to you*. And amplifying the most positive, powerful, and compelling parts of your personality really is quite fun.

However, and this may seem contradictory, if you stay rigidly fixed on what you see as your "true self," you might not realize that you can adopt different styles of behavior and still be authentic. I've spoken for many years on this concept of adapting your style of behavior in all aspects of life to meet the needs of different situations. It's what an actor does and it's been a key to my success. I found the January 2015 *Harvard Business Review*[1] article by Herminia Ibarra about how this concept applies to leadership to be important: "As we strive to *improve* our game, a clear and firm sense of self is a compass that helps us navigate choices and progress toward our goals. But when we're looking to *change* our game a too rigid self-concept becomes an anchor that keeps us from sailing forth."

People who are able to adopt different styles of behavior to suit the dynamics of a given situation are comfortable adjusting their style to different situations without feeling fake or pretending to be something they're not. It's like being a chameleon, which is different than playing roles where you pretend to be something you're not or know something you don't. Take that too far and you might start spinning the truth or even misleading people. With that said, when attempting to wow an audience, close a deal, or pitch an idea, we win when we present the *best* parts of ourselves, but not *every* part of ourselves. We succeed when we amplify the parts of our personalities that match the needs of the moment and we set aside, but don't hide, the parts of ourselves that don't.

By contrast, people who are fixated on one value system, one way of being, tend to express what they think and feel, even when it runs counter to situational demands. Doing so is not always necessary. It can be a demonstration of rigidity, the need to be right, the inability to improvise as needed, or even an intolerance of other perspectives or styles of behavior. As a result, the folks who feel compelled to express what they think and feel even when it's not appropriate for the given circumstance often have trouble performing the role required in new situations, such as moving from middle management into a leadership position, from employee to entrepreneur, from associate to partner, or even from single to married or vice versa.

Yes, I know this concept can be confounding, but if you're willing to entertain the idea that you can *authentically* play different roles and adopt different styles of behavior to easily glide from one scenario to another and one group of people to another, you may have access to opportunities that previously weren't available to you. Successful and effective people will often play different roles to suit the situation. They're willing to experiment with playing different roles until they become comfortable with the new behaviors or attitudes required to play their new parts. Eventually, each role fits them authentically and brings out their strengths.

UNDERSTANDING HOW ROLES WORK

The first principle for learning how you play the right role is to emphasize some parts of your personality and de-emphasize other parts, depending on what the professional or personal circumstance calls for. However, if you play the same role in every situation, you may cause conflict, alienate people, and limit your ability to excel.

Take the Marine Corps battalion leader. He may feel that he has to stay in character even when he's playing the role of father to his young girls. Staying in the role of soldier, he creates a home atmosphere of intensity and rigidity that creates anxiety in his daughters. Imagine if a standup comedian wanted to produce and direct a big-budget film but couldn't turn off his class-clown style of behavior in meetings with Hollywood executives. Do you think they'd take him seriously enough to let him manage all that money?

On the other hand, a college professor who understands this concept may play the role of entertaining and kindly grandfather in the classroom while taking on a much tougher role with his most talented graduate students because he wants to push them to higher levels of excellence. In my case, the role I play as a mentor to my clients is far different than the role I play as a student at my jiujitsu school. But they are equally authentic. You'll recognize me in both roles.

Tim Cook, the CEO of Apple, had already mastered a number of different roles as Steve Jobs's Chief Operating Officer. Cook coached divisions and led division heads worldwide; he cultivated and educated major retail customers; and he interacted and communicated with Jobs. When Cook became CEO of Apple, he had to learn new roles, particularly that of being the company's public spokesperson and leader of its brand. Cook now introduces Apple products in closely scrutinized presentations and meets with the most influential business and financial media. These are roles Steve Jobs once played.

On October 30, 2014, Cook did a brilliant take on a new role, a gesture that resonated worldwide. In an article published in *Bloomberg Businessweek,* "Tim Cook Speaks Up," he did something quite rare for a CEO: he auditioned for a new role and performed it brilliantly. Cook announced that he was gay and said it was "one of the greatest gifts God gave me."

Cook wrote that he did not hide his orientation. Most people at Apple knew and treated it as a mundane matter. He acknowledged that because so much of his life at Apple kept him in the spotlight, it was important to him to preserve a private sphere of his life. However, Cook found a role that was calling to him: that of socially responsible citizen. He saw that the prominence of his position, particularly as a white male CEO in a global technology brand, offered him the opportunity to provide an example that could inspire, comfort, and perhaps even protect others. He didn't do this for the stock price or to get an edge on Apple's competitors. He used the article to articulate and assume a role others hadn't expected he'd play. And the response from the LGBT community, investors, the business community, customers, vendors, fans, press, and even many political and religious leaders was overwhelmingly positive.

Cook wrote the lines for his (true) character to play in this new role: "I don't consider myself an activist, but I realize how much I've benefited from the sacrifice of others. So if hearing that the CEO of Apple is gay can help someone struggling to come to terms with who he or she is, or bring comfort to anyone who feels alone, or inspire people to insist on their equality, then it's worth the trade-off with my own privacy."

I have no doubt that a career that consisted of playing many different leading roles helped Cook prepare for this moment, but I'm sure it still required rehearsal. Cook even acknowledged how he plays different roles: "I'm an engineer, an uncle, a nature lover, a fitness nut, a son of the South, a sports fanatic, and many other things."

Here's a different kind of example. Many coaches, from Herb Brooks to Phil Jackson, also play roles that help them get inside their players' heads and motivate them to perform. Phil Jackson plays the Zen Master role to near perfection. He talks to the media, writes books, and sprinkles into talks with players and coaches his understanding of Eastern philosophy and psychology and how it applies to winning at the mental game of playing basketball in the NBA.

Most people of a certain age remember the Miracle on Ice and the improbable victory of the United States men's ice hockey team over the Soviet Union in the 1980 Winter Olympics. What you may not know is that the U.S. team's coach, Herb Brooks, consciously developed a role as part of his strategy to compete. As a coach at the

University of Minnesota, Brooks's coaching persona was that of a nice guy who supported his players. In coaching the U.S. Olympic team, however, he played an entirely different role. Knowing that the players he selected came from different college programs and had been rivals on the ice, he needed to break them down before bringing them together.

How did he accomplish this feat? Brooks became a demanding drill sergeant of a coach who pushed the players through all-night skating drills, effectively bringing them together by making them hate Brooks and his harsh style more than they hated each other. By the time they reached the Olympics, the players had bonded over their experiences and felt unified as a team. Brooks took a big risk in playing that role — but it paid off.

I'm sure there are many other examples you can think of from leaders you've admired. There are several benefits of learning how to master role-playing. You will

- Become more confident because you have a plan and the right roles for optimizing your performance.

- Become more adept as a communicator as you learn new insights to draw on.

- Learn more about yourself and your capacity to inspire and motivate.

The ability to adopt different styles of behavior and step into the right role in every situation is a potent tool for change. It's a behavior you may already use from time to time with some effectiveness, whether you realize it or not. The question is: do you want to grow and gain the value from employing this approach intentionally? I hope so. When you start identifying the roles you'd like to play and you open up to new styles of behavior, you move from supporting roles into leading roles.

ARE YOU GOING TO PLAY A LEADING OR
A SUPPORTING ROLE IN YOUR LIFE?

Let's explore the kinds of roles you want to play in your life and discuss how you can excel at them. These can range from long-term,
big-dream roles such as being a CEO to narrower, "get it done soon"
roles such as best sales closer. Perhaps you'd like to be more of a
leading man at home but less of a general at work. There are some
instances where you might want to take the leading role and other
instances when you're more effective in a supporting role. There is a
difference between being in the limelight and hogging the limelight.

Keep two important points in mind:

1. When you take on a new role, there may be loved ones,
    friends, or colleagues who aren't comfortable with your new
    role and prefer you in your old role.

Here's an example: A friend of mine left a stable job as an art
teacher because she wanted to make more money and collaborate
with people doing cutting-edge work. She started dating a man
just before she quit and took a job as a designer at an ad agency. Although her new boyfriend said he supported the move, the new corporate role made him uncomfortable. My friend wanted to become a
serious achiever and gain more independence. Apparently, her boyfriend had different plans for her.

This next statement is a bold one so I don't expect you to agree
with me right off the bat, but there may be some people you should
drop from your life. I believe that, if the people around you hold
you back from playing new and different roles, roles that serve your
dreams, those people need to go. I know that sounds harsh, it's
rarely a simple proposition, and yes, some of the unsupportive people we are tied to by blood, but you get one shot at this life and it's

your life to live, isn't it? Share it with others but don't let them write your life story and cast you as a supporting character. You are the writer, director, and star of your own life.

2. Be honest with yourself as you go through the process. Continually ask if you are trying to achieve your real goals or just trying to get people to approve of you.

For example, you may be trying to play the role of champion on your corporate team. Playing that role would make you more visible and give you a higher status in the organization, among your peers, and even in your family. However, it's important for you to remember why you are doing this work. Is it what you really want for your long-term success, or is it something you're doing for the immediate approval of the people you work with or a family member or even the Joneses next door?

You can always draw upon your collection of roles for daily life and for important performances once you have become skilled at them. They become part of your repertoire as a manager, leader, entrepreneur, parent, lover, or head of the PTA.

WHAT DO YOU NEED TO DO TO PLAY THE IDEAL ROLES YOU HAVE JUST IDENTIFIED?

This brings us to the next important question. What do you need to do to play the roles you aspire to? What kinds of performances will you be called upon to make in this role, and how will you prepare for those moments?

Here's an example from my previous career. When I left acting almost twenty years ago, I was searching for my next step. At the time, I raced road bikes, and I was teaching an indoor cycling class as a way to train during the off-season. I loved exercise, and with my background as an actor, I was good at creating motivating and theatrical experiences for the students in my class (again, playing a role).

I heard there was an open position for a group fitness manager who would be responsible for hiring, creating programming, and signing and managing the fitness instructors at one of the club locations. I saw myself in this role—I also had some new ideas for programming and a theory about why I would excel in the position. There was just one problem: I lacked any of the certifications or experience the position supposedly required.

To impress Toni, the director of the department, who had to approve me for the key interview with the vice president of the fitness division, I used my acting training to imagine myself as the perfect group exercise manager with tons of fresh ideas. I chose parts of my backstory to support my theory as to why I would excel in this position. I rehearsed how I'd present my case, and I had strong, clear motivation that I would share with them: I wanted to make group exercise the most profitable and fun division of the company (at the time it was just considered a corporate overhead). I also amped up my motivation to get that job by thinking, *If I don't get this, I won't be able to pay any of my bills, no self-respecting woman will ever be willing to date me, and I'll end up a balding, no-prospects punch line!* (Turns out I couldn't really avoid the balding part . . .)

I sat down with Toni and asked her to look at what I had done in my acting career. I explained that in the same way actors work to create memorable experiences for the audience, a group exercise class can create experiences for the participating club members. I would use my dramatic skills and theatrical know-how to make the classes more surprising and delightful. I also demonstrated that my experience with theater production was all about project management; that is, I had experience organizing people and budgets against a timeline to produce an event. And finally I told her that my training as an actor and an acting teacher made me good at identifying and developing talent as I went about hiring fitness class leaders, the best of which are natural performers.

I also pitched my theory that they were hiring the wrong characters for what the roles actually required. They were hiring top fitness teachers to be managers because of their good records in attracting students, but they weren't looking for candidates with much in the way of natural management sensibilities. Taking a chance, I told Toni: "I have an abundance of these natural talents."

I should mention that I was nervous the entire time. I don't want you to think that I just skated through the entire process. There was a lot riding on this interview and I was way outside my comfort zone. Fortunately, my training as an actor gave me the ability to control my breath and body language; a good performer can appear to be at ease in the face of great pressure, even with anxiety flowing through his veins. Toni was impressed and agreed to move me to the next step — an interview with the senior vice president of the whole division. And get this — she gave me the company's procedures manual to help me speak the language I needed to develop for my character. I studied ferociously and adopted the language from the procedures manual to fit the role I wanted to play.

I got the big job after my performance in the second interview. Shortly thereafter, I was given the opportunity to add a second club to my roster along with a salary bump of $5,000. I thanked them for the offer but declined, explaining that the math didn't make sense — it was double the work for a tiny increase in pay. This surprised them because people in the industry were usually motivated by status and approval and were willing to sacrifice themselves to get it.

So I played the role of Deal-Maker, wrote a simple script, and made a counter offer, one with a huge risk for me. "Which three goals, if accomplished within the next three months, would make you the happiest?" I asked the bosses. When they told me, I said, "I'll make you a deal. I'll take on this second club, and if I accomplish those goals within three months, you'll double my salary. If I don't accomplish the goals, I'll take the five thousand." First, there was silence in the room, followed by laughter and even a bit of snickering. But they agreed, clearly thinking I'd never succeed.

You know I wouldn't be telling you this story if the ending wasn't a happy one. I doubled my salary, and just three months after that, because I had another success while playing the role of Renegade Intra-preneur, I was promoted to director of the division with yet another salary increase. That's three promotions and almost three times my original salary within six months.

So, here are the most important steps in that experience:

1. I got clear on my superobjective and my motivation to achieve it. (More on superobjectives in Chapter 4.)

2. I decided on the role I would play, then I thought and acted *as if* I already was the great manager I'd envisioned using my imagination. (More on acting *as if* in Chapter 5.)

3. Then I drew on my backstory to fill in the role and find my voice, and I did research with the employee manual.

4. I took huge but achievable risks by making what seemed to be outsized promises while also getting things done under the radar. (More on raising the stakes and taking risks in Chapter 6.)

5. I also stayed in the moment to discover what they really wanted and needed. (More on staying in the moment in Chapter 8.)

6. I developed relationships with people who had my back and helped me accomplish my goals.

The final consideration lies in learning about your role by study-ing the best performers that you can observe. Just as athletes im-prove by practicing the shot or swing of their idol in countless repetitions, this approach can work in business roles and perfor-mances. If you see a "star" in a role you admire — say, the Master Networker — study what she does and decide what is comfortable for you to try. This doesn't mean you should pretend to be some-one else. It means learn and practice the techniques of a master per-former, just as you would in graduate school or at a seminar.

What roles do you aspire to? Would you like to move into more leading roles? If so, what kinds of performances will you be called upon to play in those roles, and do you have the courage to step into the spotlight and steal the show when you do?

Crush Your Fears and
Silence the Critics

> According to most studies, people's number one fear is public
> speaking. Number two is death ... Does that sound right?
> This means ... if you go to a funeral, you're better
> off in the casket than doing the eulogy.
>
> — *Jerry Seinfeld*

HAVING FEARS ABOUT PERFORMING in public high-stake situations
is absolutely natural. This stuff can be *scary*! I regularly have scary
moments myself. It's *how* we deal with the scary stuff that helps de-
fine who we are and how well we succeed. Our fears can be about
looking stupid, making mistakes, failing, or even just showing others that we're nervous; ultimately we're afraid of being criticized or
ridiculed. And maybe, deep down, we're also afraid of truly revealing ourselves. If someone rejects our halfhearted attempt ... they
haven't really rejected *us*, right? But if we are vulnerable and give

everything we have ... and *we* are rejected ... whoa ... what does that say about who we really are and what we're actually capable of achieving? I think it's what we most want – to be known, warts and all, and still be respected and loved.

It's natural to worry about, obsess over, or dread your next presentation, speech, interview, networking event, or even a blind date. Maybe you wrestle with questions about how to prepare. Perhaps you lie awake at night thinking about what your boss or best client will say about your next performance. It's natural to worry about how to handle public speaking situations that go wrong or even – heaven forbid – bomb. Even if these moments are relatively scarce for you, you'll benefit from this chapter, wherein I address the twin roots of the fear of public speaking: uncertainty and the fear of being criticized.

There are two types of criticism that will shut you down or make you play small: the internal kind that comes from the voices of judgment that run rampant in your brain, and the external kind that comes from members of an audience, your peers, or your superiors. As much as we'd like to avoid them, we are always going to face the external faultfinders. But we don't have to play that role ourselves and become our own worst critics.

SILENCING THE INTERNAL CRITIC

Our brains do a great job of running repeating loops of how things will go wrong when we take the stage and step up to the mic, literally or figuratively. These images and voices typically come to us from our childhood because the criticism and doubts of our parents and caregivers leave deeper tracks in our minds than many of the other "judgers" we encounter later in life (though these can come back to us as well). However, the more you pay attention to this negative chatter, the more you hear it because fear activates your stress responses.

Let's circle back to Lori, whose story I told in Chapter 1. Lori was the shy CPA who enrolled in one of my workshops in 2013 and ultimately had the courage to speak openly about her childhood, its effect on her confidence, and her desire for change. Her speech ended up bringing down the house.

Lori's voice was liberated by her accountability and honest backstory. I had taken away her note cards, so she couldn't rely on the story she'd been telling for years — which wasn't her true voice. She had to let go of the shame associated with how her mother had treated her and the false self she created as armor against that pain. Secondly, Lori had the courage to keep the promise she'd made to herself, to me, and to her peers when she enrolled in the event. She had promised to do the work to become a better speaker and find her voice. And she kept that promise. Lori's positive experience, bolstered by the encouraging and supportive crowd, is a source of confidence that enables her to share her voice more and more. In so doing, her voice will continue to grow and change. Eventually, she'll be telling a new story in a voice that is simultaneously the same and different than the one she found that day. Because she's removed this block and silenced her inner critic, she's on to a new lesson — a new story — perhaps even a new audience. Silencing the negative voices in your head is directly tied to finding the different, but all authentic, characters you can play.

Throughout the book I will continue to help you silence your internal voices of doubt, because, ultimately, isn't that the secret to successful performance in all parts of your life? If the voices in your head put you down, make you feel small, or tell you that you're not good enough, it's not likely you'll get too far. However, if the voices in your head are positive, encouraging, and supportive, telling you that you absolutely are capable of achieving your goals and dreams, you'll do just that.

SILENCING THE EXTERNAL CRITICS

Stepping into the spotlight comes with taking the chance that you'll be criticized. Just ask Bruno Mars.

The pop performer had been chosen to headline the halftime show at the 2014 Super Bowl. Part of Mars's big moment had to do with predictions building up to the performance, creating an atmosphere of anticipation that offers some instructive lessons for anyone about to experience a major speech or presentation. Prior to this most-anticipated and -watched event emerged a plethora of online media "discussions" (a charitable description of the pregame vitriol surrounding Mars's selection) bashing Mars as a baby-faced lightweight not ready for prime time. Never mind his immense popularity, a recent Grammy for best pop album, or a concert tour that grossed $72.4 million. For critics, the fact that Bruno Mars wasn't a tested commodity on a Super Bowl scale was enough to pass judgment. He wasn't, after all, a universally anointed music industry giant on par with Bruce, Beyoncé, Madonna, or McCartney. In other words, Bruno Mars wasn't a safe choice, and that made some observers antsy.

When asked about the controversy around the selection at a news conference, Bruno said, "No matter where I perform, it's my job to uplift the people. So whether I'm performing at a graduation party, a wedding, a Bar Mitzvah, the Grammys, or the Super Bowl, I'm going to give it all I got. Whatever happens, happens."[1]

That's your job — to uplift the people. Let other people pontificate on whether what you're doing is going to be a career breaker or career maker. The great performer knows that's a false either/

or. He will take the risk because the bigger the risk and the higher the stakes, the greater the opportunity to create something exciting, moving, meaningful, shocking, and inspiring. The performer knows how easy it is to criticize, so there is no point in sorting through it all. You'll be well served if you simply do your best and care more about the quality of your work than pre-performance applause or the apoplectic antagonists.

Idina Menzel played the role of Elsa in *Frozen*, the most successful animated movie in history. She also originated the role of Elphaba in *Wicked* and Maureen in *Rent* on Broadway. She might be one of the most talented and hard-working musical performers in modern history. To celebrate the new year of 2015, Menzel was asked to give a live performance of the theme song from *Frozen* in Times Square, NYC. And, boy, was it ever. On that frigid night temperatures were below freezing, more than one million people crowded the streets, and tens of millions more watched at home. She performed beautifully, until she reached for the last note.

Twitter blew up with angry critics panning her performance and ridiculing her. In response to the criticism, Menzel simply pointed the naysayers to something she'd said a few months prior.

There are about 3 million notes in a two-and-a-half-hour musical; being a perfectionist, it took me a long time to realize that if I'm hitting 75 percent of them, I'm succeeding. Performing isn't only about the acrobatics and the high notes: It's staying in the moment, connecting with the audience in an authentic way, and making yourself real to them through the music. I am more than the notes I hit, and that's how I try to approach my life. You can't get it all right all the time, but you can try your best. If you've done that, all that's left is to accept your shortcomings and have the courage to try to overcome them.[2]

She gets it. She's not just successful because of her talent. She's also successful because she is willing to do the work and silence the critics with her attitude — all in service of the audience and her art. Sure, the critics may still prattle on, but she doesn't hear them. Instead, she continues to reach for the high notes.

THE PERFORMER'S PARADOX

Criticism can arrive as potshots from the rude person in the front row or as toxic office gossip that can tear apart a team. Then there are times when a supervisor, peer, or loved one wants to give helpful feedback but doesn't know how to do that effectively. Anytime I hear, "Can I give you some constructive criticism?" I know some unsolicited and often unhelpful or nitpicky advice is about to be levied. Criticism is criticism even when dressed up as being "constructive."

Merriam-Webster's dictionary defines a critic as "one who expresses a reasoned opinion on any matter, especially involving a judgment of its value, truth, righteousness, beauty, or technique." That's a fair and perfectly appropriate way of behaving. But the dictionary also offers an alternative definition: "one given to harsh or captious judgment." That's the kind of criticism I'm referring to.

We often let criticism from people we don't know well or don't know at all affect us too much. Criticism in the realm of public speaking or any other creative endeavor taps into our more personal feelings because performing is an experience where we are undressed psychologically in public. It's a place where you're making yourself vulnerable in ways you haven't before.

A friend put himself forward for a seat on our local school board. To be selected for this volunteer position, he had to appear at a town council meeting that many parents and other stakeholders attended, and everyone was allowed to make comments for or against candidates. Anyone could say anything they liked about him. To get on the board, and to be of service, he was not only offering to donate his time but he had to be willing to be criticized, even by people who aren't willing to donate their time. He was willing because he cared more about results than approval.

Performing, whether onstage, in the field, in the office, or in a civic group where you seek a leadership position, places you under expanded scrutiny. You're stepping up and you're asking for the exposure that will result in people talking about you – sometimes negatively. The fact that your ambition to become a performer adds to your anxiety and fear and as a result increases your resistance to achieving your goal all adds to *the performer's paradox*.

As you become a performer, you will need to deal with these conflicting intentions. Your superobjective of becoming a community leader, advocate for a cause, or senior executive in a public company will battle with that familiar inner voice telling you to avoid situations where you could be criticized, laughed at, or rejected. I coach and advise many aspiring speakers, CEOs, authors, and others, and they find it helpful to realize that they ultimately have to choose between *results* and *approval*. In the end, the ones who choose results are more successful and more satisfied by their work.

Which is more important to you, results or approval? Be honest. When I was younger it was all about approval. Now, it's results. I won't sacrifice my values and certainly wouldn't ever consider hurting anyone to achieve my goals, but I don't work for applause or status. I care about helping you shine in all the spotlight moments in your life. I care about delivering on the promise of this book. If you steal the show, then I've achieved my goal.

Dealing with your conflicting intentions can also be a personal issue. In fact, many of our business problems are personal problems in disguise. That is, if you're not getting promoted at work, it might not have anything to do with your skills but everything to do with how you interact with others. You have the intention to get ahead but you might also have the intention of showing others that you're better than them in the process. Those are conflicting intentions, and they are getting in the way of your professional or personal development. If you are an artist but you can't support yourself because you won't show your work because you feel it's selling out to cater to the commercial aspects of the art world, those conflicting intentions are getting in the way of your dreams of producing art that will reach the people you're meant to serve. If you want to give speeches on a topic you're passionate about because you want to change the world in some way but you don't want to be criticized, those conflicting intentions will surely get in the way of you taking center stage. If you want to fall in love but you also want to ensure you don't get hurt, those conflicting intentions may make it hard for you to be open to new possibilities.

Or, if you are overly concerned with the approval of strangers rather than trusting yourself and the opinions of your loved ones who really know you, you are giving strangers too much power over your life and you need to stop.

If you have one intention to go out there and nail it, to steal the show, and another intention not to put yourself in situations where you can be criticized, the latter will likely cancel out the former. Now that you understand what's at stake, let's liberate ourselves from these conflicting intentions.

TWO SIMPLE STEPS TO SILENCING THE CRITICS

Step 1: Stop Being Critical

The first thing to do to silence the critics is to stop being critical. Most of us don't want to criticize others because we know how awful it is to receive negative feedback. And most of us have, to some degree, a fear of criticism. Yet many of us fall into the trap of criticizing others. Ironically, how we talk about others is also how we talk to ourselves. If you get in the habit of taking shots at competitors, venting about the boss, or gossiping, you may just derail your own agenda. Why? It's not a healthy mindset for doing your own creative work.

Most off-the-cuff criticism misses the essence of performing and public speaking anyway. Performance, or any creative endeavor, including but not limited to writing, product development, design, or project management, ultimately succeeds through an evolving process of rehearsing, iterating, and getting better through both inevitable mistakes and moments of good and bad luck. It's easy to pick out a mistake in an otherwise solid performance. Each time you pick away at someone else's work without realizing it, you are increasing the likelihood that you will do the same to yours. I don't think you can be a critic *and* a performer. I'm talking about the kind of criticism that puts people down rather than building them up. Anyone can tear something down. It's much harder — and more meaningful — to build something better instead. So, you choose ... are you going to focus on performing at your best or spend your time attempting to best other people?

By being respectful you allow other people to make their own decisions about creative work. When we judge others, we diminish ourselves. We end up playing smaller rather than bigger. Just think about it: Could a chef feel liberated doing his work while also writing restaurant reviews? Could an artist feel fully self-expressed painting in the morning and then start blogging negatively about other artists in the afternoon? I suppose they might but it suggests a serious lack of empathy. The more you criticize others, the more attention you give those critical thoughts, and the more sensitive you will become to criticism yourself. That's how the mind works. The energy it takes to compare and tear down someone else's work is lost for more productive endeavors — such as getting ready for the big speech, pitch, or interview. And, when you prepare for your performances, you don't focus on good or bad but rather on what works and what can be improved.

Step 2: Give a Presentation That Doesn't Have Any Holes to Poke

Almost everyone filling a seat, sitting in a conference room or across the table from you, is there to get something from your performance—ideas, inspiration, or an interesting analysis. Note that I said *almost*. Within that audience are three camps. Some people already support you or agree with you because you share a similar view of the world. They will continue to buy in more and more as you present. Some people absolutely will never take your perspective or have personal reasons for not liking what you have to say. You don't have much of a chance with this group. Finally, you will have folks in the middle who are open to your ideas but aren't on your side of the table yet. They may want to accept and adopt your speech's message and objective but need help or a little push to get there.

In preparing for the event, try not to focus solely on either your fans or the die-hard detractors. If you focus on the fans, you'll be heard as pandering, and if you focus only on the naysayers, you'll likely water down your message and alienate your fans as well as the large swath of folks between the two camps. Instead, focus on targeting those in the middle, whom the political scientists call the *persuadables*. They are the ones who are willing to think differently, change their minds, and potentially adopt your worldview.

Even though the persuadables are open to your ideas, you may be provoking them by asking them to change their worldview. It can be easier for an audience member, even a persuadable one, to poke holes in your work in order to escape from grappling with your ideas or opinions. That's the threshold you'll have to pass. Even the most wonderfully gracious people in your audience may try to resist your ideas or requests in order to protect their perspectives. Often, it's easier to find fault than to change a long-held belief. So it is incumbent on you to design your presentation in such a way that there aren't any holes to poke in it.

In Part III of this book, you will write, design, and develop speeches and presentations that are incredibly well organized and make a sound case for your ideas. In the meantime, let's start with a simple technique that you can use immediately to prevent others from poking holes in your point of view. Best of all, you can apply this technique to all of life's conversations and collaborations.

When I give my *Book Yourself Solid* keynote presentation in front of a marketing crowd, early on I share my perspective on marketing—that it rarely gets them clients, but it does raise awareness of what they sell. What they do once a potential buyer becomes aware of their product or service is what actually books the business.

However, I always leave room for their perspective. For example, if I use absolutes in my language, if I say marketing "never" gets you clients, then I've created holes that are easy to poke. Or, if I use other absolutes like *everybody, everything, always,* or *no one,* it's pretty easy for someone to poke a hole in my position. For example, if I say, "No one likes earwax-flavored ice cream," you could refute my theory because it's possible that someone does, as crazy as it sounds, like earwax-flavored ice cream.

As you read this book, notice how I always attempt to leave room for alternative ideas or experiences, by qualifying my statements with, "it seems like . . ." or "it is often the case . . ." or "it appears to me . . ." See what I just did? I said, "I *attempt* to leave . . ." because it's possible that I may inadvertently use an absolute that isn't actually an absolute somewhere in this book and miss it when editing. It's unlikely you can close every hole, but do everything within your power to make your arguments solid. If you do, it's less likely you or your work will be criticized. Plus, all generalities are false. Including that one.

THANK YOU, BUT NO

It's sophisticated to reflect on and analyze what's working and what can be improved in all aspects of your life. It's the key to successful personal and professional development. Additionally, it's helpful when someone offers you reflective, thoughtful analysis and tailors the discussion in great detail to what you want to achieve rather than their own agenda. It's mature and usually the most productive for them to ask consent to share their opinions and ideas with you. It's smart when they pick the right time to offer feedback (five minutes after your presentation is not that time).

However, unless you are professionally or personally obligated to take someone's feedback, you have every right in the world to say "Thanks, but no thanks" when it's offered. Too often we let other people inside our heads to be polite or out of some self-imposed sense of responsibility to hear people out. I don't think you have to. Of course, I don't suggest closing yourself off from feedback; just make sure you allow in only the thoughts of conscientious and caring people.

When you feel anxious about an aspect of a performance, always focus on the right thing—achieving your objective. Your job is simply to deliver on the promise built into the content of the speech you've created and rehearsed, the product launch you've shepherded through channels, or the annual strategic planning session you've designed and will facilitate. Always focus on the outcome you want to achieve in a meeting, interview, or negotiation rather than how you think you're doing and what you think people will think of you.

RISE ABOVE THE NOISE

Returning to the advice of our friend Bruno Mars, while you and I might not be movie or music stars and may only give a game-changing performance a few times a year, our job as performers is to uplift the people, to rise above the noise, and to give our audience a powerful experience that will change their thinking about their work, ignite their passions to make a difference, believe in something new about themselves, or say *yes* to your request for a salary bump, *yes* to buying your product, or *yes* to investing in your company.

Don't give critics the chance to slow you down — and don't let the critic inside you do that either.

part 2

POWERFUL
PERFORMANCE PRINCIPLES

In Part I, The Performer's Mindset, you discovered that the whole world is, in fact, a stage and that you can write and play your own hero's story. You now know how to crush your fears and silence the critics, play the right role in every situation, master authenticity in performance, and find your voice to step up and speak out.

Now, in Part II, Powerful Performance Principles, I'm going to teach you the principles you'll be able to use for all of your public speaking and performance situations. In just a few short chapters, you'll learn how to amp up your motivation so you will achieve all your objectives; use the power of your imagination to act *as if* so you can increase your confidence and step out of your comfort zone to play a bigger game; say *yes, and* . . . so you're more creative and compelling to be around; be in the moment so you can respond to all the crazy things life and your performances throw at you; raise the stakes so you make your performances more exciting; and choose early and often so you never sit backstage, vacillating over whether to take the spotlight or not.

Once we've completed Part II, Part III offers A Master Class in Public Speaking, which is about creating and organizing your material for speeches and presentations; using improv to shine in all performance situations; taking Q&A like a pro; deploying humor to lighten the mood and to move others; creating dynamic audience interaction so people stay engaged; finding and telling great stories to enthrall and enrapture; mastering rehearsing so you're ready to go at a moment's notice; performing; and much more.

4

Have a Clear Objective

You should always have an objective. Often in a good script, an
objective is written into the scene: to end the affair, to propose,
to move out. Your action can change from scene to scene but you
should always work out what you are meant to be doing.

— *Dee Cannon, acting teacher*

THIS FIRST PRINCIPLE IS ABOUT CHOOSING where you want to go,
what you want to do, and what you want to accomplish with your
performance. In acting terms, we refer to our most important goal
for a performance as the superobjective and the smaller goals that
get us to the big goal as our subobjectives.

In order to reach this big goal, you'll need to try every tactic you
can think of until you succeed. You'll need boundless amounts of
motivation to drive you forward toward success because obstacles

are sure to stand in your way. That motivation is made up of your underlying needs and wants: I need food. I want money. I need security. If one tactic doesn't get you what you want, you try another, and if that doesn't work, you'll try another, and so on.

Think of it like working on a project. The project is designed around a big goal or a deliverable (the superobjective). Then, you identify the milestones (subobjectives) that you need to accomplish in order to achieve the big goal. Once you have milestones, you figure out which tasks (tactics) you need to pursue in order to reach them. If you have a deep need to achieve the big goal, you'll try any task you can think of to get it done.

In any given performing situation, by defining your goal, you are able to uncover your true motivation. If you're making a speech, going for a promotion, trying to secure a loan, or interviewing for the job of your dreams, your motivation has to be so strong that you will not leave the room until your superobjective is achieved. For example, classical music conductor Benjamin Zander said in his TED talk, "The Transformative Power of Classical Music," "I'm not going to go on until every single person in this room, downstairs and in Aspen, and everybody else looking, will come to love and understand classical music. So that's what we're going to do."[1]

Let's say you're going to give a speech to highlight the work of a charity you've become involved with and sit on the board of. You're passionate about the charity's work and have waited for years to get a leadership position. Your *why you do it* could be that, by the end of your speech, every person who hears you will make a contribution — including that Wall Street financier you imagine at the back of the room who will see you afterward and hand you a check made out to the charity for $250,000. Your deep need to achieve this goal is driven by your motivation to save lives, and that informs your choices (the tactics you'll use) for the character you'll play that night. This is a technique. Please don't take the example literally – don't filibuster the room until the audience falls asleep, chases you off the podium, or you make everyone donate even if they don't want to.

From speech-making to networking, motivation is a powerful and liberating tool available to guide you in the decisions you make. This might sound easy, but in practice many of us lose sight of our motivation to achieve a particular goal because of fear, distraction, or disillusion. During my acting training, I was taught to ask myself during early-stage character development and rehearsals: *what are my goals and what is my motivation to accomplish those goals?* And so should you, no matter what you do.

Where many go astray isn't so much in their lack of motivation – after all, we are all motivated in some way in every circumstance. The fault lies when our objectives and/or motivations are unclear, conflicting, or muddy because we haven't approached the question with a true, clear purpose. Think about job interviews or presentations that fell short of your goals. Were you razor-sharp about your objective and was your motivation mission-critical – or were you focusing on what you think someone else wanted to see?

Another example of the importance of having strong motivation can be seen in something that happened at a wedding. It was a tale of two toasts. The first one didn't have a clear goal or much discernable motivation to achieve a goal. The second had both.

We were sitting at our tables, settling into our dinner. The father of the groom gave a flat, vague, and unfocused toast. His speech was written on a few loose pages that I had seen him editing right before the reception. He said some nice things about the couple, he wished them well, related a few memories about his son, thanked people for coming, and then free-associated a little about going out on your own. He lost his place a couple times in his speech and wasn't able to express the joy he really felt inside.

His objective may have been to simply give a good toast, but that's a losing proposition. You can't do a good job without a clear objective and compelling motivation about the other players in your scene — *what you want for them or from them* — and then acting out *as many tactics as needed to achieve that goal.* The father's motivation could have been to make his daughter-in-law feel that she was now not just his son's girlfriend but an essential member of the family. To successfully do this, he needed some kind of motivation that would drive him and guarantee he'd achieve this goal. Why was this goal so important? What's the backstory? Was his son widowed and the family adored and can't stop talking about his first wife? Is the new wife often made to feel like she's an outsider by other members of the family? How important is it for the father to make his son's new wife feel like family? He may have had this intention but it didn't come through in his performance — and this is key — because he didn't think through what he wanted to achieve in the moment and how he was going to get there. So his speech fell flat. He also didn't rehearse. Objectives and motivation are keys you uncover during the rehearsal process.

On the other hand, at the same wedding, the bridesmaids had written and rehearsed a joint toast that stole the show. I knew they had a clear objective and strong motivation that got them started with their big idea. They wanted to give the guests a true understanding of what it's like to know the bride and groom the way *they* knew them — as great friends; as a real couple; as *people,* not two figures on top of a wedding cake. They created a clever stage bit about a dictionary that included definitions of all the terms that describe the couple. They performed it like an old-school comedy routine, with one bridesmaid throwing out the term and then another delivering the laugh line. They even created a mock dictionary that they used as a prop and gave to the couple as a gift.

This was certainly the kind of toast that could have gone badly, but they had rehearsed so much that they owned their material. They were funny, bawdy, and loving. They stole the show. Their idea came out of their objective to share the real people they knew the bride and groom to be, and it worked.

HOW DO WE GO ABOUT
FINDING OUR MOTIVATION?

In the same way the actor needs to think through the writer's motivation for creating the characters, you need to know the goals your boss or event sponsor or negotiating partner has for the job at hand. If you are doing something on your own, know what you're trying to achieve and why. The actor will plan and study how her character will take action and respond minute by minute through the play. She will think about how the character responds to success, adversity, or bad news. In your process, you want to think about how your choices move you toward your objective — or not. You want to think about how you respond to specific criticisms, how you overcome specific objections you expect to encounter, and how you will respond to any anxiety-provoking challenges.

When making choices, always start with *why* and continue to ask yourself *why* until you get to the root of your need or desire. If you do, you'll unleash a motivation so compelling that you'll do everything in your power to pursue it. And that's what will make you interesting to watch. When you give a speech, if your motivation is clear and you'll try every tactic you can possibly think of to achieve your goal — do everything in your power to get the audience to think, feel, and do what you want them to do — then you'll be inspiring to watch, gratifying to hire, exciting to date, thrilling to love, and just too darn fun.

USING QUESTIONS TO ESTABLISH MOTIVATION

Discovering motivation starts with asking the necessary questions. Many acting coaches teach a variation of legendary Russian actor and director Constantin Stanislavski's questions for character development. I've adapted them to serve your needs so you can use them to prepare for any pitch meeting, job interview, speech, or even first date:

What do I want? If you're giving a speech, and you don't have a strong objective, what's the point of being there? You're not there just to have a pleasant conversation. What is so important to accomplish that you must take the stage, so to speak, in order to accomplish it?

Why do I want it? You must always have a strong reason for pursuing your objective. And when I say *strong*, I mean it is something you must accomplish at all costs, a save-the-world kind of motivation.

What will happen if I don't get it now? The stakes should always be high. Otherwise, so what? The consequences of failing to achieve your objective need to be too terrible to do anything but achieve your objective. Ambivalence is never interesting, cool, or compelling.

What happens if I do get it now? For you, the rewards must be so compelling that you're willing to do whatever it takes to achieve your objective. For the audience, the rewards must be so compelling that they're willing to change the way they see the world, to say *yes* to you, to think what you want them to think or do what you want them to do.

What can I do to get what I want? This question leads you into the crucial distinction between knowing how to *play* the line and how to *say* the line. We'll explore this further later in the book, but keep in mind the infinite ways there are to say and present the same words depending on your goals and circumstances. You need to work out how you are trying to affect the other person with what you are saying. And so it is with speech-making, deal-making, and dating.

What must I overcome? You must have an inner and outer obstacle. The outer obstacle gives the resistance (usually another person, company, industry, or social pressure) to attaining your goal. The inner obstacle is your own mental conflict. In speech-making, the resistance in the audience creates conflict; we can't impose our perspective in a speech. Asking people to change the way they see the world can feel confrontational to them. It's a lot to ask in a short period of time. You need to overcome that resistance to reach your objective. The same is true in sales. The buyer often pushes back, offering great resistance. His objections are the obstacles you need to overcome. The same is often true during a job interview. The interviewer may have objections to hiring you that you need to overcome.

SAVE ENERGY AND SHARPEN FOCUS

Another benefit of knowing why you do it: you simplify your actions and make fewer wrong turns. You can map out how your performance carries out your motivation to achieve your objective. Having specific objectives and clear motivation means you know what you should not do, so you don't waste mental or physical energy. When we're doing too much at the office, in relationships, or onstage, it comes in part from not knowing what we want and where we're going. One of my business partners, Matthew Kimberley, often says that feeling *overwhelmed* is not necessarily a function of having too much to do but rather not knowing what to do next. By identifying one superobjective for a performance or critical situation and mapping your plan to reach that superobjective, you are freed from much of the fear or anger or other emotional baggage that can be churned up in these situations.

The above questions will help you prepare for the spotlight. You'll know your objective and you'll be deeply connected to your motivation. You'll go after what you want with calm, focused, and steady abandon. And, guess what? You'll achieve your goals.

5

Act "As if . . ."

I believe in imagination. I did *Kramer vs. Kramer* before I had children. But the mother I would be was already inside me.

— *Meryl Streep*

MOST OF US HAVE EXPERIENCED IT: that antsy feeling that we're out of place or insecure in certain social, public, or personal situations where we're the center of attention. We can't find that mental release from our discomfort, even when we are in the midst of an opportunity that interests us — whether a date or a speaking opportunity or a job interview. We hear the inner voice saying, *This is not you,* or maybe a voice of authority from our distant past saying, *You really don't belong here.* That sense of not fitting in or being ready for the spotlight is a reality the vast majority of us face at one point or another, but there is a way to control this feeling. We turn to our second principle, which actors call acting *as if.*

WHAT IS ACTING *AS IF*?

Acting *as if* is an imagination technique for converting what we see as adverse circumstances in work or life into new and more aspirational opportunities. When you are acting *as if,* you are using your brain's amazing powers to positively anticipate and create a different way of seeing the world and/or a different way of behaving. It's a technique that helps overcome negative behaviors and attitudes that hold you back so you can begin to make more conscious and intentional choices about how you want to perform and what you want to achieve when it matters. In the words of Mark Twain, "You cannot depend on your eyes if your imagination is out of focus."

Here's another way to think about it. The word *drama,* according to the *Oxford English Dictionary,* derives from a Greek word meaning "to do" or "to act." Therefore acting *as if* gets you ready to take the initiative. It starts you thinking about your intention and the possibilities ahead. Most actors agree that acting *as if* learned early in their training is a magical elixir for inhabiting the challenge of developing a character. It helps them focus on what that character wants to achieve. Then they start thinking *as if* they were that person, *as if* they lived in that time, *as if* they were in the character's situation. Most actors use this principle to begin the process of filling in a multilayered understanding of a character, often drawing on nothing more than their life experience, some research, and, most profoundly, their imagination.

You can certainly adapt this approach to help find and secure the manner in which you want to be perceived as a speaker at a public event. Even better, by adapting this technique, you'll find that you can catapult yourself into a higher-level performance.

WHY AND HOW TO ACT *AS IF*

But how does one get into the mindset to act *as if?* How do you master this technique? One key is in understanding "disclosive spaces." This may sound academic but there are great insights to be gleaned from this concept.

A disclosive space is the way each of us sees the world and operates in it — our personal perspective, but more than that. It is our way of understanding how different complexities are interrelated, how they fit together, and how we fit into them. Children can rarely understand things outside their own disclosive space, but as our brains mature we develop the potential to see and understand in depth things that are outside our own experience, if we simply pay attention. A nonperformer might look at the spaces outside him- or herself as separate and apart, while the performer sees these disclosive spaces as opportunities he or she can step into, inhabit, live, and portray.

Imagine you and a colleague have a conflict over a work-related issue. You think he went behind your back and spoke badly about you. You confront him about it and he says that he's the one who's been betrayed because you didn't give him the benefit of the doubt. It doesn't matter who's right and who's wrong. But if you can't say, "I'm going to look at this *as if* I were him," then how can you resolve the conflict?

As adults we allow our disclosive spaces to narrow as we become so busy or caught up in our daily activities that we neglect other points of reference and unique perspectives. Our sense of disclosive space is also affected by factors such as mood and mindset. I'm sure you've noticed how being in a good mood makes it easier to notice the people around you and take an interest in them while being in a bad mood does the opposite.

The *as if* technique can help you use your imagination and life experiences to inhabit disclosive spaces as part of your journey to achieve your goals. It's a way of being mindful of other people and circumstances and incorporating that knowledge into how you live and work. Events such as speeches, team meetings, or networking get-togethers teem with new disclosive spaces to inhabit.

ACTING *AS IF* ON THE JOB

I think about my acting friends who had jobs in retail during their early years of training and starting out in theater. One of them was a greeter at Bloomingdale's who had to stake out high-traffic parts of the store and steer shoppers to the various departments. Even if she had a long night in rehearsal or just wasn't in the mood, if she was going to keep her day job, she had to be absolutely convincing that she was delighted to be there and in service to the people coming through the door. If that's not acting *as if,* I don't know what is. Acting *as if* got her ready to shine every time. She imagined the shoppers *as if* they were classmates of hers from college at a reunion on one day, *as if* they were her favorite group of cousins another day, *as if* she was a part owner of the store the next day . . . whatever *as if* helped her tap an outgoing generosity and keep her mind engaged and playful so she could perform at a higher level.

I'm not suggesting you have to be someone else to act *as if.* Sure, there have always been a few great method actors who behaved *as if* they were actually the character offstage or between takes. I love the story about the filming of the epic thriller *Marathon Man,* when the great method actor Dustin Hoffman found himself exhausted after staying up a number of nights in a row just as the character in the script does. His counterpart in the film, Sir Laurence Olivier, was considered the greatest living actor in the world at that time, and he did not go to those extremes. One day, legend has it, Olivier turned to Hoffman, who was nodding off on the set, and said, "Why don't you just try *acting,* my boy?" I like to think that Olivier wasn't putting him down. Rather, he was trying to relieve Dustin's stress by showing him another perspective, another way of being.

THE POWER OF IMAGINATION

I started this chapter talking about imagination. Learning to act *as if* is not about visualizing idle fantasies about wealth and power. Acting *as if* is about using the brain's amazing powers of imagination to learn, change, and experience new things. The majority of mental health professionals and neuroscientists say this is healthy, because you're refocusing the brain on productive pro-social and contributory behaviors; it can also be transformational.

There's a bookshelf of research on the effectiveness of imagination and cognition to improve one's athletic performance, overall health and well-being, and even aging. Research on visualization shows that imagining the execution of a task successfully contributes to more positive outcomes. Brain scans support this by showing that visualization triggers a shift from the left to the right brain hemisphere. This transfer from the left (logical) hemisphere to the right (creative imagination) hemisphere enhances visual imagery and actually creates new neural patterns in the brain.[1] "When an athlete visualizes success, their body really is experiencing success," observes Dr. Bernie Siegel, the author of *Love, Medicine, and Miracles* and retired professor of surgery at Yale Medical School. "When you imagine something, your body really feels like it's happening."[2] Acting *as if* is just that — strategic imagination aiming you in the right direction for successful personal and business performance.

HOW WE CAN USE ACTING *AS IF*

Acting *as if* is also a strategy for dealing with anxiety and worry. It helps us stay balanced and organizes our energy. It's one of the ways you'll reduce stage fright, which can occur anytime you're in the spotlight – be it when you are leading a meeting, giving a speech, being interviewed, or even docking a boat. I have a decent-size boat, and even though I'm a United States Coast Guard–licensed captain, it can be pretty tricky to dock a boat when weather conditions aren't favorable, so I visualize the entire process before I start. This works like a charm. I imagine that I'm going to dock the boat in this slip *as if* I've done it ten thousand times. Most good old salty captains with whom I've talked about this tell me they do the same thing – even though they, in fact, really have already docked the boat ten thousand times.

By acting *as if* you begin to shift your consciousness from self-defeating ways of thinking into new conscious directions. It may seem simple in its approach, but the power of positive visualization lets your brain "rehearse" what lies ahead so that when your big performance arrives, it will seem *as if* you have already done that speech thousands of times before. This is what rehearsal is for.

The acting *as if* technique is one to keep handy for emergencies as well. It can be surprisingly helpful in difficult but ultimately manageable times when you may not be at your best, coping with a personal issue or even just dealing with a lingering cold. But using an *as if* approach will work when you know the show must go on.

You know how body language affects how others see you, but it may also change how you see yourself. Harvard University social psychologist Amy Cuddy has done extensive research on how "power posing," standing in a posture of confidence even when you don't feel confident, can raise testosterone levels while reducing cortisol levels in your brain. In fact, Cuddy's research paper, "Power Posing: Brief Nonverbal Displays Affect Neuroendocrine Levels and Risk Tolerance,"[3] published in 2010 by the Association for Psychological Science, showed that various power poses increased testosterone levels by 20 percent and decreased cortisol levels by 25 percent. That's a pretty dramatic representation of the power of acting *as if.* In fact, Cuddy's motto is, "Fake it until you make it," which you now see actually has biological implications. Of course, the best part is that you can do it authentically.

As with any sustained commitment to learning new ideas, the more you invest in acting *as if* and the other performance techniques, the more these ways of being will translate to gains in your public interactions. "The mind, once stretched by a new idea," Ralph Waldo Emerson once observed, "never returns to its original dimensions."

The act *as if* technique gives you the opportunity to become the thing you're imagining yourself to be. You act *as if* you're in charge. You act *as if* you are calm. You act *as if* you look forward to speaking to large groups. And slowly, those things become more and more true. And your performances become more and more natural.

Your imagination is a powerful asset. If it can make you *think small,* it can also ensure you *think big.* If it can make you *feel small,* it can ensure that you *feel big.* Eventually, acting *as if* becomes acting *as is.*

Raise the Stakes

LEARNING HOW TO TAKE THE RISKS required of winning performances and to manage any anxieties or fears you have in the process
calls for becoming comfortable with discomfort. This means you
first figure out what kind of risks to take and how they will benefit you. Then you start getting comfortable with the discomfort
that risk-taking brings. Sometimes that means breaking the rules.
No, I don't mean you should break rules that will get you fired or
incarcerated. Rather, adopt the principle that to create memorable
presentations and performances, sometimes you must find ways to
surprise, delight, provoke, and push the boundaries of your audience to build and create new things.

Let's say you're responsible for a presentation about your unit at
an annual meeting, and in the past you've used PowerPoint and have
done a competent, vanilla-sugar-cookie kind of job: to the point,
brief, factual, and professional. But others at your level do the same
thing and even you know it's boring. Your teenage kid suggests you
try to produce a video like DollarShaveClub.com — something funny,

quirky, and memorable. While you may be unfamiliar with video and nervous about surprising your boss, you decide to take the extra time to hire a young producer to create a two-minute documentary about your team's greatest accomplishments as the characters from the TV program *The Office*. Since you're not going to play it safe and produce a typical "industrial" corporate video, you don't want your boss to say no or start micromanaging the video, so you get it completed under the radar.

You know the results you're looking for: Your team's work will be more talked about and remembered than in years past. You will also demonstrate that you can use technology and, more importantly, creativity, to improve the audience experience. Even if your boss or peers find fault with the video, unless it is stupidly offensive they won't be able to do more than quibble and will most likely be blown away by your commitment to making it happen. But that's the risk you take. Outstanding performers learn to take smart chances even when they're scared.

HOW TAKING RISKS PAYS OFF

Now, please don't lose your perspective on this. Don't take risks for the heck of it or for a short-term gain such as showing up a competitor or getting flash-in-the-pan publicity. Risk levels and results must correlate. Let's say you're a small-business owner negotiating for the first time with a large company that is offering a substantial contract but their deal terms are particularly unfavorable for you. In many situations like this, the small business may take the contract as offered to "bag the elephant" and get the hefty contract even if the deal terms don't sustain profitability.

With your new mindset of a performer, you can raise the stakes by simply sitting without speaking or moving after you make your counteroffer—which can be really uncomfortable. If they reject it, you can simply get up, thank them for their time, and leave the room. It's simple. It's dramatic. *And it's risky.* You've got to be willing to walk away. But, they may call you back in and tell you they had time to think about it and are happy to accept your offer. Or, you may not get the contract. But there are also considerable benefits to establishing a precedent for future business, ensuring your big contract can be performed profitably, and perhaps, best of all, by building your confidence. This is a performance, remember: you're stepping out of your role as the quiet, compliant small vendor to act *as if* you are on the same professional plain, *as if* you have the confidence to negotiate for what's fair and what a qualified vendor should have in this situation. Win or lose, you know you've stayed true to your values and didn't sell out. But, most times, the outcome will be a better contract and a better prospect for success for the risk taker — that's you.

DISCOMFORT OFTEN SIGNALS OPPORTUNITY

Before I started my own business, as I mentioned earlier, I was an executive at a publicly traded sports club company. When I came onboard, the company's financial systems for payroll and reporting were a disaster, particularly for assessing the value of fitness instructors and, most pressingly, for getting these same instructors their paychecks. I knew if I didn't make immediate changes, I wouldn't be able to keep top performers and evaluate payroll per instructors vs. club revenues and profits. Surprisingly, after meeting with my boss, I found out the leadership didn't want to make any investments or major overhauls.

The choice was clear — keep my head down and make very little impact (and start looking for a new job) or raise the stakes so I could make life easier for myself and the employees and produce better results for the company to boot. The first option would be comfortable and easy, the second option would require living with the knowledge that my job could blow up quickly. I shared my concern with my girlfriend at the time, and she told me she knew a fellow in her tech department who was a whiz at financial modeling and who created software on a freelance basis. So I traded him two executive club memberships for a piece of financial software that he developed per my specifications. I showed it to the leadership team and even though they weren't thrilled that I flew under the radar to get it done, they loved it and rolled it out companywide. If they hadn't loved it, I might have looked bad and suffered a setback. That was the risk. But I also knew the goal was worth it. Three months later, I received a promotion. Coincidental? Absolutely not.

Remember: You're not taking risks just to take risks. There's a reason why you're performing – to produce better results professionally and personally. And when you dare to get bigger results, this can be the most exhilarating and personally satisfying aspect of being a performer.

By raising the stakes, you adjust to being comfortable with discomfort. As you rehearse for your conference speech, wedding toast, sales pitch, or plan how you will negotiate your deal, you experience discomfort and allow yourself to feel uncomfortable so you can find out what happens when you work through the idea. I remember this experience well from the writing and rehearsal process for my show, *The Think Big Revolution*.

See what I just did there? I referred to *The Think Big Revolution* as a "show." I perform it as a fifty-five-minute keynote at conferences across industries and to different demographics. But, I don't think of it as a speech or a talk. Instead, I think of it as a *show*. Doing so allows me to think like a performer rather than a speaker. It encourages me to *show* rather than tell. It compels me to take more risks and make bigger choices for the audience.

There's a scene in *The Think Big Revolution* show when I talk about raising the stakes and being comfortable with discomfort. I tried on the idea of wearing a pair of red 6-inch-high heels during the scene to demonstrate being comfortable with discomfort because it made me both physically and emotionally uncomfortable. I knew the audience would never forget the point. Would the choice work or would I look like an idiot? I didn't know. But, instead of saying *no* to the idea, I took the time to rehearse it to see if it would work. If it did, I'd keep it in the show, even if it made me uncomfortable. After all, the job of the performer is to serve the audience, no matter how uncomfortable he or she is during the process. After kicking the idea around for a few weeks of rehearsal I took it out of the show because I found a better way to illustrate the concept. However, I would never have ultimately found a better way of doing the scene and nailing my point had I played it safe from the beginning.

RAISING THE STAKES FOR BETTER PERFORMANCES

Pushing the comfort zone is what great performers do well — because time and again they discover that by playing all out in rehearsal they find the smaller or more refined choice that brings the character to a new level. In Marlon Brando's famous audition for *The Godfather,* he took the chance of stuffing his cheeks with cotton because he wanted Don Corleone "to look like a bulldog." It worked so well that not only did Brando get the part but Francis Ford Coppola re-created the look for the character with a plastic prosthesis.

Another way of raising the stakes is making a promise to your audience. The promise has to relate to something that matters to you and is reflected in your subject matter. And the promise is something you've worked through in your rehearsal process and are confident you can deliver. When President Kennedy said in an address to Congress, "I believe that this nation should commit itself to achieving the goal, before this decade is out, of landing a man on the moon and returning him safely to the earth," he was making a promise and raising the stakes for his administration. If you're making an annual presentation about your department's objectives for the year and you start the speech with a declaration that by the same time next year you will increase net profit from 9 to 15 percent — you will have the attention of everyone in the room. (Yes, yes, yes, you absolutely have to have a smart strategic plan to actually make this kind of promise.)

Let's be real: it's a scary world when you're performing instead of watching. If there weren't risks in performing in high-stakes situations, the rewards would be far fewer. It may feel like you are balancing on a high wire with people torn between wanting to see you fall and wanting to see you cross safely to the other side. But that's all in your mind. *Most people, especially an audience, don't want you to fall.* They want you to take risks so that it feels to them like you're balancing on a high wire, but all the while, they're rooting for you to make it to the other side successfully. If you can do it with some flair and a bit of panache, they'll stand up and cheer for a job well done. When you complete the high-wire, high-risk act with grace, you've won the room and the crowd.

Say "Yes, and . . ."

WE ALL KNOW THAT FAMOUS SAYING, The show must go on. Well, here's the rub about that old chestnut: The show never goes on when you say *no* in any area of life. Whatever the personal relationships among the cast members, when they are rehearsing and performing, actors (and performers, creative artists, inventors, and visionaries) thrive on the power of saying *yes*. Saying *yes, and . . .* not only improves the writing and rehearsal process, but it makes meetings more effective, helps persuade your spouse or partner during a difficult conversation, and gives you a new confidence for networking and winning the room.

In her book *Bossypants* and in many interviews, Tina Fey of *Saturday Night Live* and *30 Rock* fame has explained the importance of saying *yes* in her work and then figuring out how to do what she agreed to later. "Whatever the problem, be part of the solution," she writes. "Don't just sit around raising questions and pointing out obstacles."

Know the distinction between saying *yes* and giving lip service. Saying *yes* is about having the mindfulness to recognize and to respond positively to the content and feeling of another person's thoughts in conversation in real time. Saying *yes, and . . .* is about a leap of faith where you give your attention to what others are offering, trusting that you'll know what to do next.

THE DANGER OF SAYING *NO:*
SHUTTING DOWN CREATIVITY

Let's say you and I are doing an improv scene for an audience and you come onstage limping, clearly in a lot of pain, shouting, "I've broken my leg!" and I respond by saying, "No, you haven't." Suddenly, the forward momentum stops. I've shut you down and the scene might not carry on. However, if I responded by saying, "Oh, my goodness, that's terrible! But, your hair looks fabulous. Did you do something different with it?" Now we're onto something because I've framed my reaction by saying *yes, and . . .* You would be able to respond in many different ways, one of which would be, "Really, do you think so? I was at the hair salon and the stylist used so many chemicals that I passed out, fell out of the chair, and that's how I broke my leg."

This principle doesn't apply solely to improv (I'll explain more about using improv in Chapter 14). As a strategic tactic, saying *yes, and . . .* helps us to look at creativity, collaboration, and problem solving as a way to maintain momentum regardless of the negativity or problems that come our way.

THE DANGER OF SAYING *NO:*
DISCOURAGING AUDIENCE ENGAGEMENT

How does this tactic apply to performance or public speaking? One bestselling author had finished his speech and was taking questions. An audience member asked: "How can I meet the most relevant people at this event?" The speaker didn't like the question because, rightly so, he thinks everybody is relevant. However, he then humiliated this poor guy by telling him so in front of thousands of people. The energy in the room deflated as the audience members suddenly realized that they too could be ridiculed. After that, only a few more people mustered the courage to ask a question, and I'm sure many left with an enduring negative impression of a bullying moment, rather than appreciating the good advice that was present inside the *no* that surrounded the answer to the question.

A more helpful approach might have been to bridge from his question by reframing it: "Thanks so much for your question. Yes, it reminds me how everyone here is relevant, so I'd recommend spending as much time as you can networking because you never know how one relationship can open the door to another." The author could then pivot and offer advice on how to meet people. The simple reframe would have recognized the individual asking the question and also served the audience. The point is, there's always a way to turn a potentially negative situation into a positive forum by using the *yes, and . . .* technique. Yes, it does take a little time and forethought to do this, but it can and should be done, especially if you're eager for a warm reception at the end of your talk.

THE DANGER OF SAYING *NO:* PREVENTING CREATIVE DIALOGUE

Is there a person in your workplace meetings or teams who likes to take the role of devil's advocate (such an unappealing cliché when you think about its meaning)? Let's call him the DA. You know how he works: As the meeting develops, a colleague puts forth a suggestion or initiative. Invariably the DA plays his part. "Just to be the devil's advocate," he begins, "here's why that won't work," or "Gary in accounting won't go for it." And so on. What's inevitable is that he shuts people down, slows down the positive flow, doesn't bridge to the workable aspects of the idea but continues to poke holes in it. In fact, the DA loves to poke holes in things and even relishes the role. The DA justifies his advocacy with statements such as, "We can't take off with a half-baked idea." The truth is, just as there are no fully baked cakes that don't pass through a half-baked stage, the same applies to ideas.

The deeper truth is that your colleague is saying *no* far too many times. Monitor these kinds of conversations as I have and you will notice how quickly the overall productive and collaborative discussion will die off as the meeting leader moves on to the next routine topic. The DA has, in effect, killed off creativity and shut down dialogue. If by any chance you've played the DA or can influence someone who does, consider this if you want a more prominent role in meetings and want to become a shareholder of more successful ideas. When a peer at the table makes a suggestion and the DA interrupts and sees issues with it, redirect the energy of the room. Realize that being the party of *no* hurts the DA and the people around her. Shift the discussion by using the *yes, and* . . . tactic and you'll begin gaining allies and collaborators.

Saying *no* happens often and you don't want it to happen to you. Talented people who say *no* to the spotlight tend to stay in the background, behind the computer screen. The more they say *no,* the more comfortable they become with the status quo and the more they are upstaged — allowing people to steal the show from them.

SAYING *YES, AND* . . . PERFORMING
WHEN THE STAKES ARE HIGH

If you have fifteen minutes to spare, listen to Michael Massimino's audio story produced by the nonprofit storytelling organization *The Moth* (as broadcast on many public radio stations). Massimino is an

MIT-trained astronaut who was assigned to take a spacewalk to fix one of the Hubble Space Telescope's most valuable and delicate technologies, a spectrograph that detects whether atmospheres on far-off planets in other solar systems could support life. Talk about pressure ... Massimino, working with another astronaut who is inside the shuttle, examines the sensor, which was designed to be tamperproof, in a rocket-scientist kind of way. His fellow astronaut talks him through different solutions as one idea after another fails, but they never say *no*.

Massimino observed, "I was beginning to feel pretty alone and I don't mean sitting in a chair by yourself on a Sunday afternoon wearing your slippers and reading the newspaper alone." The two astronauts have the fate of the Hubble Space Telescope in their hands and they keep saying *yes, and ...* to one more idea and one more thought and one more approach until the sensor is fixed. Finally, Massimino enjoys a moment watching Earth hanging amidst all of the terrifyingly beautiful grandeur of space from outside the shuttle.

HOW *YES, AND . . .* WORKS FOR YOU AT WORK

Saying *yes, and ...* is key to the way many of our greatest entrepreneurs think and work. Google executive chairman Eric Schmidt said in a much-admired speech to UC Berkeley's graduates in 2012, "Even if it is a bit edgy, a bit out of your comfort zone, saying yes means that you will do something new, meet someone new, and make a difference in your life, and likely in others' lives as well. Yes lets you stand out in a crowd, to be the optimist, to stay positive, to be the one everyone comes to for help, for advice, or just for fun. Yes is what keeps us all young. Yes is a tiny word that can do big things. Say it often."[1]

But Schmidt didn't just start talking about *yes* in his commencement addresses. Saying *yes* pervades Google's famous culture and operating processes, which are not quite the corporate fairy tale imagined on the street but are nonetheless innovative and dramatically different from life at many competing tech giants. Many of Google's processes are about keeping up manager-employee dialogue, personal enterprise, and access to senior executives throughout the organization free of unnecessary *no*s. Among the many examples at Google are its TGIF meetings, where employees submit public questions to senior management; posting employee and team quarterly goals on its intranet; its flat and flexible organizational structure, where employees are allowed to change projects without going through approvals; and its practice of allowing its employees to use 20 percent of their time to develop and explore their own initiatives.

Tim Ferris, author of *The Four-Hour Work Week,* is another example of how the saying *yes, and . . .* mindset can power you past the conventional boundaries. Tim decided to keep saying *yes, and . . .* over and over again to his big idea that it's possible to be successful by working fewer hours, not more. He persevered, despite enduring early failures. Supposed experts and gatekeepers said *no,* but Tim and his literary agent, Stephen Hanselman (also my agent), kept saying *yes, and . . .* until they finally got the green light from one publisher. Just one. And that's all they needed. I'm sure those who said *no* are still kicking themselves because, at the time of this writing, *The Four-Hour Work Week* is fast approaching sales of nearly 2 million copies.

NEUROSCIENCE BACKS SAYING *YES, AND . . .*

Saying *yes, and . . .* is also confirmed by science as a tonic for your brain and productivity. I won't get too technical, but if you haven't heard about "negativity bias" it's a pretty interesting concept. Experts in neuroscience write about this frequently. Because our brains evolved millions of years ago, when human beings could become a meal for a lion or saber-toothed tiger or be easily overrun by marauding tribes, survival required noticing the faintest signals of danger in our environment. Over the millennia since, we've become wired to scout for danger. As a result, our brains tend to have greater memories, stronger initial reactions, and more stickiness for the kinds of *no*s and pushbacks that are common in an office workplace and in business in general.

The parts of our brain that fear serious mayhem are easily triggered by small stuff, such as the boss shooting down your idea in a meeting — dinging your tribal status in front of your peers. As neuroscientist and author Rick Hanson has written: "We continually look for negative information, over-react to it, and then quickly store these reactions in brain structure. For example, we learn faster from pain than from pleasure, and negative interactions have more impact on a relationship than positive ones. In effect, our brain is like Velcro for the bad but Teflon for the good."[2]

Because our brains have this almost telepathic paranoia for criticism and threat, scientists and neuroleadership experts such as David Rock have written about the importance of avoiding the brain's threat radar in managing and motivating people (including yourself) to give their best performance. Performers know this intuitively.

When people encounter a stimulus, Rock has written, "their brain will either tag the stimulus as 'good' and engage in the stimulus (approach), or their brain will tag the stimulus as 'bad' and disengage from the stimulus (avoid). If a stimulus is associated with positive emotions or rewards, it will likely lead to an approach response; if it is associated with negative emotions or punishments, it will likely lead to an avoid response."[3] Numerous studies show that the engagement we get from focusing on the approach response has positive effects on decision-making, stress management, collaboration, and motivation. Or as Rock says, "people learn best when they are interested in something. Interest is an approach state."[4]

Saying *yes, and* . . . is an approach trigger—it begins the *positive* cycle of creative, productive problem solving. Saying *yes, and* . . . isn't about giving yourself permission to say or do whatever crosses your mind. But it is about giving yourself permission to explore and experiment, to improve your ideas by finding out what works and what doesn't. As I'll show in Part III, writing and rehearsing for your spotlight moments can be messy, and you need to say *yes, and* . . . to your own talent so it can find its way.

If you really want to take the first step to becoming an outstanding speaker and performer, then get accustomed to saying *yes.*

Be in the Moment

LISTENING IS A DRAMATIC TECHNIQUE you can use on a daily basis. But what actors mean by *listening* is probably different from what you're familiar with. Listening is about fully inhabiting the moment with other rehearsed and prepared cast members so that they respond to the scene with choices that are authentic, fresh, and consistent.

When actors are not listening in this way, they are not responding to what is actually coming back at them and they will seem inauthentic, which leads to disjointed and disconnected performances. Listening is about bringing *all* your skills to the performance. Rehearsal prepares you for the performance. If you're prepared, during your performance you will be able to listen to what is actually happening around you; it helps you stay in the moment. What you do when you're on live is what people will remember — and listening is a powerful component of live performance.

We like to think we listen to what others are saying but I'm not sure we listen as well as we think we do. Have you had conversations where, mentally, you've already written your script and are running through it in your mind while the other person is talking? I know I have. Instead of being interested in actively responding to what you hear, you're looking for a place to jump in with your own script and score a point. But by honing my acting skills over the years, I've improved my ability to truly listen to what is being said. Not just to *understand* but to *feel* what's being said. Listening is one of the most underappreciated tools in the performers' toolbox. Great actors don't manufacture emotion. They get angry, sad, or joyful in response *to what they hear.*

Cicely Berry of the Royal Shakespeare Company, in her book *Voice and the Actor,* says, "In his relationship with the other characters [the actor] must give himself up wholly to listening so that what they say can affect him. It is only by being this open that the voice will respond freshly and that it will be surprising. It can then take the actor himself by surprise."[1]

There are four ways the most connected people actively listen:

- Thorough preparation;
- By being present;
- By paying attention with all their senses;
- By viewing themselves in the third person — using aesthetic awareness.

PREPARATION FOR YOUR OWN PERFORMANCE

When you *prepare* for a pitch, meeting, speech, or negotiation, the goal is to know your material so well that you are free to be in the moment. This is an important condition for listening because it's hard to allow yourself to improvise if you don't know your material right down to the core.

Rehearsing gives you the confidence to respond to the events and reactions of the moment, knowing you can come back to where you want to go with your planned content. You'll be able to respond without disallowing anything outside of your predetermined script. When you're interviewing for a job, sitting down for a meeting with the executive team, or meeting someone for the first time, if you don't know your material well, it can be difficult to stay in the moment because much of your brain's bandwidth is being taken up trying to remember or figure out what to do next. However, if you know your material so well that you can purposely "forget" what you prepared, you can bring new riffs, changes, and higher energy levels to your performance. You know your material so well that you can stay in the moment and let it come to you organically. Or consider what happens when I meet editors in the publishing industry to talk about a book project. I can be extremely well prepared with my pitch, but if I'm not open and ready to respond to suggestions and comments I receive during the meeting, they may decide I'm not an author they want to work with because I'm not open to their ideas. So I always approach these meetings with my mind very alert and open to how the people in the room are responding to the book discussion. Since I'm well prepared, when the editorial team offers new ideas and suggestions, I'm comfortable going off-script and confident that I can go back to my script, adjusting as necessary. But it all starts with being well prepared and rehearsed so I can stay in the moment and listen to what's being sent my way. Being prepared increases the odds of seizing big opportunities in the moment.

PRESENCE

Presence is the second facet of listening. In the midst of a performance, whether you are sharing or alone in the spotlight, presence is about using the power of silence and pauses to stay rooted in the moment as it occurs. When you're not speaking, you want to really concentrate and hear what's being said, as opposed to quickly jumping ahead to your next response. This habit requires its own level of persistent practice to tune in to using your senses to slow down and absorb the verbal and nonverbal language of your counterparts. You'll never have a particular moment again, so it's worth the investment to fully experience it in real time.

Presence helps make you a "whole brain" listener with greater empathy and engagement. Improving presence improves individual communications. The auditory neuroscientist Seth Horowitz, author of *The Universal Sense: How Hearing Shapes the Mind,* wrote in the *New York Times,* "Listening is a skill that we're in danger of losing in a world of digital distraction and information overload. And yet we dare not lose it. Because listening tunes our brain to the patterns of our environment faster than any other sense, and paying attention to the nonvisual parts of our world feeds into everything from our intellectual sharpness to our dance skills."[2]

Fortunately, you can train your listening — it's a skill like any other — if you focus on improvement, that is. Train yourself, when listening, to clear your mind of anything other than what is being said to you. Don't plan your response. Don't judge what you're hearing. Don't just listen to the words. Listen for the emotional undercurrent, listen to the confusion in the thought process, and to the pacing and tone and inflection, and you'll actually *hear* what's being said.

This is why later in the book we'll also focus on managing the pace and speed of your speech. If you are speaking without pausing, it's likely that you're not listening to what the audience needs from moment to moment. If you are always talking, you aren't reacting. And our reactions are hugely powerful aspects of communication.

Backstage columnist Craig Wallace, who has written frequently about presence, says, "Real listening [is] the kind that requires you to clear your addled mind and focus exclusively on the person right there in front of you and what he or she has to say, the kind in which you allow the person's words and thoughts to penetrate your heart and mind and then let your reactions to those words emanate purely and powerfully from your eyes as your face relaxes from its neutral curtain and becomes alive with expression. Real listening is about listening as a form of communication that is just as dynamic as speaking and is appreciated as such."[3]

Presence isn't just a practice for actors, Zen monks, or yoga teachers. Think of professional athletes and the ability certain players have to get into the zone (to inhabit the moment that allows their skills to be fully expressed with effortless flow unhampered by any distractions) and stay in the zone no matter the distractions. When I'm giving a speech, I can actually watch myself doing it. An amateur may walk offstage and say, "I have no idea what I just said." But a professional knows exactly what she did every step of the way. Not only is she performing, she is actually observing her performance in real time. This is a powerful experience. It's a high-level skill that you will develop over time. You don't need to be a professional to do so.

PAYING ATTENTION WITH ALL YOUR SENSES

When you are present, you also begin *paying attention with all your senses*. Consider a deal meeting or job interview where you are entering that particular room or office, most likely for the first time. You want to notice: What is the size of the room? What does your counterpart's desk or table suggest to you? What is the layout of the workplace? What are the other people wearing? If you're being interviewed by an executive who looks exhausted, makes poor eye contact while slurping a massive cappuccino with a half-eaten sandwich on his desk, these are all real facts that you should notice as they will affect your performance. If you walk through a workplace and notice people moving briskly, exhibiting confidence and energy, grouping up informally for a casual meeting, this is valuable data as well.

Listening isn't just something you do with your ears. When I am giving a speech, in addition to observing myself, I'm listening to the audience with my ears, eyes, and body. When I see people taking notes, I know they're resonating with a point I made and I know that I need to pause so they don't miss what I'll say next. If I sense a touch of fatigue or feel they're getting restless, I'll get them up on their feet and have them play a game (you'll learn more on audience interaction in Chapter 13). If there's a glaring technical glitch, I'll openly address it. If it's hot in the room, I'll try to fix it. Showing empathy for the audience means I'm paying attention to how *they* are listening and what *they* are feeling. It's the difference between awareness and a lack thereof. If you're not aware that your mic is too loud or if there's no mic and you're speaking too softly, you'll lose the room pretty quickly.

Think of this heightened approach to listening as a long-distance kind of pitching and catching. Let's say you and I are having a "long toss," so to speak — talking one-on-one but we're fifty yards away from each other. After I say my lines, as a listener I will wait to see if you "caught" what I said — and that means not only seeing the ball hit your glove but listening for the *thwack* sound. I will then pause to ensure that you have caught the ball before I continue. The same technique applies when speaking to a small group of people or even a large audience. In short, listen to your audience and give your words some time to sink in before going on to your next point.

AESTHETIC AWARENESS

As you become a more accomplished performer, you'll be ready to move on to a more advanced stage of listening that involves *aesthetic awareness* — a performer's sixth sense of how they are being perceived and how their audience is responding as they use the stage, deliver their presentation, and interact with the people and situations around them. You can do this in a job interview or negotiation or any of life's important performances. Experience and dedication result in a new ability; you will see yourself as the audience sees you. As I mentioned above, an experienced and well-rehearsed performer sees, feels, and hears everything that's going on in the room around her and can also *see* herself while she's performing. It's the ability to keenly observe yourself while you're in the moment. It may be a hard concept to grasp when you haven't experienced it, but if you focus on the techniques I'm giving you to stay in the moment, you'll eventually know it yourself. It's powerful.

Choose Early and Often

You always have two choices:
your commitment versus your fear.

— *Sammy Davis Jr.*

THROUGHOUT THIS JOURNEY, use the courage of your convictions to make strong choices. It's the actor's secret weapon for surprising audiences and creating dramatic moments. And it's yours too. It's fine to make wrong choices based on good intentions, but if you fear making choices — to the point that you fail to make them at all — it can be fatal to your performances. Why? For many people, self-doubt and procrastination are the twin enforcers of the behaviors that have already prevented them from taking the next step.

I've found that one of the big obstacles people face in seizing opportunities for speeches and other public expressions of leadership is an unfounded fear of making the wrong choice. However, if you don't make big, sometimes risky choices, your performances will be as unique and exciting as Wonder Bread. Only by making strong choices will you experience success and progress and therefore reinforce your commitment to change yourself and the world through your work and performances.

This principle is quite compelling to me because it is a common skill exhibited by the most successful people, and it is within your reach. Making good strong choices isn't being smart or wonderful. "It is our choices . . . that show what we truly are, far more than our abilities," author J. K. Rowling has written.[1] Making choices is simply a skill to learn and a technique to apply.

Above all, don't procrastinate. You'll never catch any fish if all you ever do is debate with yourself about which type of bait to use and never throw a line in the water. You won't likely discover your superobjective, clarify your motivation, say *yes, and . . .*, take risks, learn to live in the moment, and act *as if* unless you make strong choices and put them into play.

Yes, it takes courage to make strong choices. I know many people who are prone to procrastination, are aware of it, and work hard to overcome it. I also know many people who have been hurt by it: sales opportunities wasted, deadlines missed, loves lost, plans mislaid, and careers destroyed.

Not adopting the commitment to choose early and often can hold you back at every step. For example, when I was an actor and my agent would call me with a scheduled audition time, I'd head to his office to pick up the script and find out which scenes the casting director had assigned me to prepare. I'd hoof it over to Starbucks, fight all the other actors for a free seat, hunker down, and read through the script. As I began work on the pages assigned for the audition material, I'd start to think about what the casting director, director, and producer might be looking for from the role.

Anticipating what they wanted and aiming to deliver that rather than making my own choices about what I thought would be most compelling was my first big mistake. Unfortunately, I didn't realize this until years after I left acting. It was a *thonk*-myself-on-the-head kind of moment. *I had it all backwards.* In reality, the casting director, director, and producer wanted me to come into the room and show them how the role *should* be played — how *I* thought it should be played. The casting director wants you to do a good job because he doesn't want to be fired.

Casting directors are replaced faster than Elizabeth Taylor's husbands when the director isn't happy with the actors she's seen. How do they solve that problem? Just bring on a new casting director, of course. The irony is that the new casting director, for the most part, just brings in the same people. It may seem like there are a lot of actors out there, but in reality, there's only a small group of actors in LA and NYC that actually get the auditions. The director wants you to walk into the room and show her how this role should be played. Why? It makes her life easier. She's got so many things to contend with, the last thing she wants to do is to tell you what choices to make when creating the character. Furthermore, during the audition, she may be thinking, "I hope this actor doesn't ask me any questions about how to play the part," because even though the studio is giving her fifty million dollars to make the film, it's her first feature. She's previously only shot music videos and never had to direct actors at this level. Of course, this isn't always the case, but often it is.

It's the performer's job to go in and make big, strong choices, to show the decision-makers and your audience that you have a viewpoint, a perspective, that you're willing to take risks and push the limits. Because even if all of your choices don't work perfectly, they'll at least know that you are someone who makes bold decisions, early and often.

This is your job too. When you are tasked with planning the family vacation, choosing the restaurant and related activities for a first date, interviewing for a job, organizing content for a speech, or any other activity that requires choices, it's your job to make those choices expeditiously, with as much clarity and boldness as possible. Show the recruiter that you are willing to make choices and have a strong point of view. Show your prospective love interest that you have a vision, not just of what you are going to do on your date but of your future also. Show an audience that you have an agenda and are clear about why you're on the stage and what you're there to do. If you can do all of this while being flexible and adaptable, changing when the situation calls for a new perspective or way of being, you'll be a top performer in all aspects of life.

I do my best to work this way with the members of my team. I don't tell my director of operations what to do all day long. We set out goals for the year, for the quarter, for the month, and even for a particular week, and it is her job to make the choices that will produce the intended results. For my creative team, we choose the direction and I give them the parameters and the results I'm looking for. I then expect them to make strong choices and produce results. But I don't tell them what choices to make unless they ask for help, then we collaborate and make choices together. It's not complicated. It takes guts. I only hire people with guts, by the way. I'd rather work with someone who oversteps perceived boundaries from time to time than someone who won't put one foot in front of the other.

If you don't make choices early and often, it's unlikely you're going to get the kind of spectacular results you want.

CHOOSE EARLY — BUT NOT ALWAYS QUICKLY

Follow a few basic rules when making choices early and often. First, so I'm clear: I'm not suggesting you start making a display of activity or make changes when you are *really* unsure. Your decisions don't have to be perfect; by making them, you learn what works and doesn't work so the next choice you make will be better. In the same way, taking risks is rooted in knowing the difference between dumb risks and smart ones.

In his book *Blink,* Malcolm Gladwell famously popularized the psychological model of "thin slicing" judgments and decisions based on minimal amounts of data and lifelong experience. Gladwell uses the example of John Gottman, a well-known marriage expert who claimed he could prove, within an hour of observing a couple, with 95 percent accuracy, if the couple would stay together for at least fifteen years. The application of thin-slicing to our discussion lies in the scientific basis of the reliability of your own knowledge and experience when you make choices.

When you are in a new field or subject area or a totally unfamiliar environment, it makes sense that you will be more deliberate in your choices until you gain confidence. Keep in mind that when you choose *early,* you are often overcoming reluctance and the fear of making a decision; choosing *quickly* is simply making the decision, no matter what the outcome.

In the hiring process, for example, the consequences of your choices affect other people and even the viability of your team or business. This decision-making process should unspool until you have met and vetted enough candidates and had other stakeholders interview the finalists. Rushing this sequence would be *fast;* making the offer as soon as you are confident you have enough data and are comfortable would be *early.* I just hired a new assistant. She was willing to go through a two-month interview process. I made the choice of whom to hire slowly but I chose to bring on a new assistant early. I didn't wait until I was so far into the weeds that even the best executive assistant in the world would have a hard time helping me recover.

THE MYTH OF UNDERPREPARATION

Finally, choosing early and often is the heart of the rehearsal process, which you'll master by reading Chapter 12. If you're not choosing, you're not preparing. The best performers in the world are ready to go before they walk onstage. Some may joke around with the prop master a moment before their entrance, others may sit quietly in a corner, and others will be bouncing up and down on their toes to pick up their energy, but they're all relaxed in their own way, and they're ready to go. They've rehearsed effectively; they've made their decisions ahead of time. They're not making their choices during the performance. They're not winging it. As a result of making their choices ahead of time, they're relaxed at showtime. And, more importantly, they're not dreading the performance. On the contrary; they're *excited* to perform.

That may be the biggest difference between performers and other individuals who are worried about their performances. Performers can't wait to get onstage. Others are somewhat intimidated, nervous, or even scared about walking up to the podium or looking into a camera, in large part because *they're not prepared*. They haven't made big, clear, bold choices in preparation for the moment.

Furthermore, there are still executives and leaders out there who promote the myth that they don't need to prepare or rehearse because they're so good on their feet. Nine times out of ten, show me someone putting their slides together the night before a presentation, and I'll show you a procrastinator who has not overcome his or her fears and anxiety about performing. Having seen hundreds of underprepared speeches, I can easily analyze them for the numerous ways their lack of rehearsal shows through and undermines everything that moment could have meant for them.

It takes far more courage to start choosing, writing, and rehearsing early – courage that I know you have today.

part 3

A MASTER CLASS IN
PUBLIC SPEAKING

SO FAR, you've learned that you're willing to overcome your fears; silence your critics; use role-playing to excel in numerous different scenarios, personally and professionally; and play bigger than you ever have before. You've discovered six powerful principles that are an internal operating system for all performance situations. You've begun to see performance from a different perspective because you've adopted the performer's mindset.

As I mentioned in the beginning of the book, I intentionally started working with you from the inside out — with the more pressing issues of fear, anxiety, role-playing, and finding your voice — rather than from the outside in, which would just have layered technique on top of a nonperformer's perspective.

I've asked you to change the way you see the world. I've asked you to change the way you do things. I've asked you to think bigger about who you are as a performer. By now you realize that you don't have to be an entertainer to be a performer. Most importantly, you've discovered how to use the actor's craft to shine in all the performance situations in your life.

Now it's time to get down to the nitty-gritty. I will show you the how-tos and the what-not-to-dos along with the protocols and processes for creating, rehearsing, and nailing speeches and presentations. My promise to you is this: the techniques in Part III can help you give noticeably better speeches and presentations.

How to Craft Captivating Pitches, Speeches, and Stories

THIS CHAPTER IMPARTS STRATEGIES for creating content that will take you from blank page to polished content for a range of performance situations, from speeches to small-group presentations and even job interviews. As with the rest of the book, you'll read a lot about giving speeches, but my program will work for any type of professional or personal content you prepare. I will show you how to make a pre-performance plan, organize content, and master creative and effective writing practices.

Most presentations require an effective content creation process. However, let's not think of it as speechwriting but rather as a creative process for organizing your ideas into a compelling performance that delivers on a promise. And don't worry if you think you don't have any talent for writing. Take comfort in the words of Edgar Rice Burroughs: "I have been successful probably because I have always realized that I knew nothing about writing and have merely tried to tell an interesting story entertainingly."

You may be an experienced writer, familiar with the cycles of creation and revision; you may write speeches and presentations when needed but don't see this as a particular strength; or you may write an occasional email and that's about it. I'm not here to evaluate your grammar (there are no bonus points in public speaking for knowing whether to use a comma or a semicolon – as I'll discuss later, the spoken and written word are not necessarily the same). I'm here to give you a method that removes fears, questions, and doubts about preparing first-rate material you believe in so you can deliver it in the spotlight. When you have something important to say, you find the words.

As you're working through this chapter, please consider:

- **Which aspects of the writing process tend to be the most difficult for you?** Is it getting started and generating ideas? Is it organizing your ideas into a structure? Is it knowing how to find, craft, and tell stories?

- **What types of superobjectives will you have for the speeches and presentations you give?** Selling a service? Promoting the performance of your team? Recruiting new investors? Raising awareness for a cause or industry? I see it again and again: one of the most common mistakes in performing is losing sight of the true objective in order to get the audience's approval.

- **Give the development process enough time.** You'll be glad you did. Very few people realize or recognize that creativity is an iterative process. There may be a few people on this planet who create perfect content on their first pass, but I haven't met them.

- **Once again – remember that most of the methods I describe in relation to speeches transfer to many other types of performances.** Just as you devise a three-act structure for a speech, you can develop a three-act structure for a monthly review meeting that you lead.

THE THREE ESSENTIAL ELEMENTS OF EFFECTIVE CONTENT CREATION

Element One: Getting Ready

Well in advance of a public performance, start the content development process with a simple five-step exercise. This will be useful as a reference going forward, and as a warm-up to loosen your creative muscles so you can begin to give them a workout. Please answer the following questions:

- **What type of performance are you going to give?** Is it a forty-five-minute keynote speech? A twenty-minute department review at a sales conference? A reading from your book? A fifteen-minute pitch for investors? A software demo? An interview? A product pitch?

- **Who is the audience for the performance?** Who will be in attendance? What are their interests and concerns? Will you be addressing seven hundred public school teachers expecting an educational speech? Will you be leading a webinar to show off your new product line? Will you be giving a toast at your son's wedding?

- **How will your audience benefit from the performance?** Will you be educating, motivating, selling, or raising awareness, or a combination of some or all of the above?

- **What is your call to action?** What do you want the audience to do with what you've shared and how do you want them to feel about it?

- **How can you leverage your performance?** How can you repurpose your content or material, if applicable? Can you turn this ten-minute talk into a longer keynote-type address? Can you turn this product demo into a webinar/streaming video Q&A session?

Now, let's get down to organizing your content, shall we?

Element Two: Organizing Your Content

Excellent public speaking can be used to promote your big ideas and to change and transform the way people think, what they feel, and what they do. Your performance can save the world. Literally. If your performance results in one person in the room making a positive change in his life because of you, well, you've changed the world. If your performance results in a big sale that will make your company so much more successful that it will create more jobs and allow you to hire new employees, you've changed the world. If your toast at your son's wedding makes his new bride feel like a member of the family, you've changed her world. If you educate an audience about the importance of preventive care and one person schedules a screening that catches a major health concern, you've saved her world. My public speaking training company isn't called Heroic Public Speaking for nothing. Our goal: *to save the world, one speech at a time.*

If you want to have world-changing impact, this goal requires a well-informed plan anchored with a big idea. Then you need a framework for getting your audience to the big idea, and you need to choose the right structure for organizing the content. (The expert doesn't always know that much more than the novice. The expert is often perceived as an expert simply because his information is better organized.) Then you'll discover how to reorganize and repurpose your big idea speech or other performance for different lengths and different purposes.

Hey, What's the Big Idea?

A big idea supports the promise of your speech. Sure, it's the main point you want to make, but it's also a statement of conviction that takes a position on whatever your topic may be. A big idea shows to the audience the world as it is, and it shows them how much better the world could be if your idea became a reality – that's the promise of your speech. It also demonstrates how much worse their world will be if they don't adopt this new way of thinking or being.

Why is this important to public acts of persuasion and communication? Because you're asking the audience to change views they may have had for twenty, thirty, forty years or more, and our human inclination is to find reasons not to listen rather than being made to feel uncomfortable. If you want them to listen, your message needs to contain a big idea they can believe in along with a promise that that big idea gives them the results and benefits they're looking for.

Your big idea might be provocative. Your idea may challenge what audience members believe about your particular topic and why their point of view could be flawed. Your performance should not be needlessly or gratuitously offensive. It can be controversial simply because the topic is provocative, but it doesn't have to be.

Nor does it need to be original, as long as your big idea is rooted in your overall expertise and beliefs. Remember what I shared earlier: *you don't need to be different to make a difference.* Well, the same goes for your content. It doesn't necessarily need to be different to make a difference. Keep in mind that this big idea is the foundation for your entire performance. It delivers a big promise to the audience. Yes, it's an idea, but an actionable one.

Your big idea doesn't have to tackle issues of international importance; it can animate a technical, sales, or business subject such as changing software platforms or adopting a new marketing approach. These are often big issues for you and the people around you and, as a result, are life-changing.

Let me share some examples across a spectrum of speeches and situations. Note the performance and the big idea. Google the speeches I list below and study them. Pay attention to the way each speaker performs. How does she use her voice and speech to create dynamic contrast? Does he use props or visuals? How does she structure her content? And, of course, make note of anything else that strikes you as effective.

- Dr. Martin Luther King Jr.'s "I Have a Dream" speech: America's promise of freedom and opportunity for whites and blacks alike will not be realized until true integration is achieved.

- Elie Wiesel is a Holocaust survivor, human rights activist, and the author of *Night* and fifty-six other books. The big idea of his powerful 2011 commencement speech at Washington University: where there is injustice and persecution, do not stand idly by.

- Jill Bolte Taylor's TED talk, "My Stroke of Insight": She tracked her brain after a stroke and through an agonizing recovery; in the process she discovered that we are hardwired neurologically as much for peace and connectivity as we are for linear thinking.

- Oprah Winfrey's 2008 commencement address at Stanford University: More than many want to admit or realize, great decisions come from listening to your gut and following your inner wisdom.

- Susan Cain's TED talk, "The Power of Introverts": Rather than asking introverts to change, we should embrace their qualities to become more effective human beings.

- Seth Godin's TED talk, "The Tribes We Lead": The Internet is facilitating new social opportunities for ordinary people that recall the strengths of ancient tribes.

In each of these speeches, the performer articulated the promise behind the big idea and how the audience would benefit by listening and paying attention. However, no matter how world-changing your big idea, the audience must connect the dots between the message and the messenger. Connection won't be possible if your audience doesn't understand why you are a credible messenger and why your message has to matter to them.

Let me give you an example: In one of my seminars, a young U.S. Navy officer was working on a keynote speech about domestic violence perpetrated by soldiers on their spouses or partners and approaches for reporting and stopping these behaviors in the military. For personal reasons, he wouldn't reveal why he had chosen to deliver this speech. Therefore, no one in the seminar could understand why the officer had taken ownership of this topic. Had he committed abuse and was making amends? Was his sister a victim of abuse? If he'd only been able to discuss the situation a little more openly and share why this topic was so important to him, the audience would have understood and seen him as an impassioned messenger.

The following questions will help you develop and evaluate a big idea in any particular situation:

- What matters most to you? What are you passionate about?

- Could this change some aspect of the world for the better?

- What is your personal connection to the subject matter?

- What does the world of the audience look like in terms of this idea? What are their limitations, concerns, hopes, and dreams?

- What are the costs of *not* changing?
- Finally, what is the *promise?* What will the audience get out of listening to you? What will the world look like if the audience adopts your big idea? (Remember, "audience" can simply mean one person sitting across a desk from you.)

Now frame up your content.

Framing and Organizing Your Big Idea

When you organize the way you think and write for your audience, you organize the way they hear your idea and think about it. That's a great service for your audience, whether it is two venture capitalists or an auditorium filled with colleagues. It also helps you give the presentation. The better organized it is, the easier it is for you to remember the structure and content. Remember back in school when you were taught to write your outline before you wrote your essay? Do you remember all the good reasons your teacher gave you for doing that? Structure is even more valuable now. In those days, it might just have been about getting the grade. Now you're creating content that has high stakes for your life; frameworks sharpen your focus on the most important findings in your material.

Thankfully, you can organize your ideas using a few information blueprints that have worked for countless nonfiction bestsellers, keynote speeches, group presentations, panel talks, and lectures. These frameworks become trusted companions as you prepare for your next spotlight moment. They give you the map-making tools to lead your audience to your big idea and through underlying themes. They can also be combined and used together. I'll use books as examples rather than speeches because it's more likely people have read the same books than have heard the same speeches.

- **The problem/solution framework:** Dramatize and illustrate each problem and then offer a compelling solution. Your framework alternates problem with solution and your prescription for addressing the solution, weaving in stories and data, and building up to a big result. Politicians often use this structure. (FYI, it's not the framework that makes some politicians seem phony. The framework is benign; it can't hurt a fly. You only come across as phony when you *are* phony.)

- **The numerical framework:** Well known to consumers of business books and speeches, the numerical framework is an old standard. Maybe you're familiar with Steven Covey's *The 7 Habits of Highly Effective People*. This framework has been used and reused countless times. The reason it is put to task so often is because it works. Numerical frameworks allow you to break up a number of recommendations or new ideas into easier-to-understand chunks. Your numbered sections can be keys, principles, elements, rules, or values. You can deliver the key points in any order, in most cases. The numbered points will always lead up to your big idea.

- **The chronological framework:** Present information in sequential order based on time or logical consistency, going from past to present to future. *Your Pregnancy Week by Week* by Glade Curtis is one of the bestselling books in history and it uses this structure. Steve Jobs's epic presentations introducing iPods and iPhones used sequential structures, pitching one feature at a time and leading his audience to understanding the latest release's features.

- **The modular framework:** This is the framework I used in *Book Yourself Solid* and *Beyond Booked Solid* (along with the chronological framework), which means you can use the book sequentially and learn my program in order, but the sections are also modular in that they can be read and applied separately. You can go to different modules for the information you need now rather than reading the entire book.

- **The "compare and contrast" framework** is best suited to a discussion of two major subjects or thematic points where you'll be showing differences. It's one challenge to compare and contrast the role of intellectual property in the U.S. and China and another to compare and contrast the same topic in ten other countries. Jim Collins used the compare and contrast framework effectively in his book *Good to Great* and in the hundreds of speeches he's given based on it. Collins and his team analyzed more than 1,400 companies, identified eleven that became great, and then compared and contrasted the variables that led to the eleven standing out over all the rest.

- **The three-act structure:** Aristotle's famous three-act structure can work as a framework for your speech. I'm talking about the story arc universal to theater and drama of situation-conflict-resolution. Many plays and movies have three acts built on this structure. The situation (act one) presents the given circumstances of the world; in a business speech, for example, you establish the status quo, such as the current product line. Tension and conflict arise (act two) when obstacles come between the speaker or character and her objective; in a business scenario, the obstacle might be that popular products are falling out of style and the division is losing money. Resolution arrives (act three) when the speaker or character successfully overcomes the obstacle; perhaps the sales issues are resolved by proposing market-tested new products to revive sales.

The Two Types of Speeches

The frameworks apply to all types of content, but here's an additional important category to keep in mind with speeches. They will mostly fall into two types — *curriculum* (content or informational) and *idea* (message or experience) speeches. You will choose which general way to go based on the format and expectations of the speaking event, and what works best for who you are as a performer and your superobjective for the speech. Choose the curriculum speech for a prescriptive educational purpose — such as my *Book Yourself Solid* keynote or the introduction of a new manufacturing protocol. Your curriculum speech should provide detailed recommendations for a business management speech, or prescriptive steps for change for a self-help or advice speech. To be clear, curriculum speeches have strong messages and big ideas. Otherwise, you wouldn't create them.

The message speech isn't generally that prescriptive, as it inspires, motivates, and energizes with an informed perspective or a new code to live by. A wedding toast is a message speech. Many of Seth Godin's talks and my *Think Big Revolution* speech offer good examples as well (you can look up both on YouTube.com). Most TED talks are message speeches. However, you should know me by now: I don't believe there is just one way to do anything. Don't get overinvested in the frameworks and types. A message speech will often offer a protocol or include intellectual property, and a curriculum speech should certainly contain a big idea and inspire people. I simply give you these frameworks so you can use them as a way into the creative process.

In fact, the speech I deliver as the keynote for this book doesn't follow any of these frameworks. Instead, it's an entertaining and educational play that I perform with Amy, my partner at HeroicPublicSpeaking.com. We call it *Steal the Show: A Keynote in One Act,* and it allows us to teach the content and put on a show at the same time. Now, I don't expect you to perform and write a play to get your message across. We're professionals, it's our job to challenge the status quo and to put on performances that walk the thin edge of innovation in our industry. Although, you may surprise yourself; maybe you have the talent and desire to perform some skits at your next quarterly report meeting. Keep an open mind, grasshopper . . .

Reorganizing and Repurposing Your Material

You know how much better you feel as an adult when you tackle one of those imposing household duties — such as reorganizing the basement, filing all your paperwork, or holding a yard sale to finally get rid of those old Parcheesi sets, punch bowls, and cross-country skis you're never going to use — and suddenly it's so much faster and easier to deal with important issues? That's similar to the payoff you get from putting the time and extra rehearsal into my method. You will have tightly written, well-planned content anchored in big ideas — content that's so solid you can easily repurpose it for a variety of situations.

You will always do the research and make the adaptations needed to steal the show for whatever event you're participating in. But now you're operating on a different level than many of your colleagues who scramble to write something for every need. You can expand message speeches into content workshops, or condense a content workshop into the message speech at its core.

A three-part, sixty-minute keynote can be reorganized into a twenty-minute TED-style talk by delivering only one of the modules. That same sixty-minute keynote can be expanded to fit a three-hour workshop. When you use a numerical framework made up of seven keys, you can teach them all or you can teach a few. When you use a problem/solution framework, you may share some of the problems and solutions with people on your team, whereas you may share all the problems and solutions with the executive committee.

Element Three: Creative and Effective Content Creation

This third element gives you two for the price of one: it provides step-by-step advice for transforming your presentation or performance blueprint into the written word, and it helps you refine your own working process so it best serves your mental health and professional goals.

Please know that speeches don't have to be written out word for word, and if they are, they certainly don't have to be memorized. Instead, you can create an outline with key points, supporting points, stories, and more. But that doesn't get you off the rehearsal hook. Both types of preparation require just as much rehearsal.

I teach some of my students to write and memorize speeches. They learn how to perform with spontaneity, authenticity, and ease; the audience feels like the entire speech was crafted in the moment. Others prefer to follow the structure outlined above and improvise their way through the framework (which is not the same as winging it). They often use sticky notes to organize and memorize all the various components of the speech: key points, stories, audience interaction, calls to action, and more. To do either well, rehearsal is required. I'll show you exactly how to rehearse in Chapter 12.

In the meantime, use these seven steps for creative and effective content development and writing. Then we'll explore the importance of using contrast.

1. **"Brain dump" everything you know on the content topic.** The goal is to tap your creative and associative powers without activating the judgment and censorship of the linear brain. Start out with a session of freeform writing or speaking, just to get it all out. I usually do this verbally and have someone take notes for me, but you can also opt to make an audio recording.

2. **Organize the brain dump by compartmentalizing related ideas.** Look for the main points and supportive material and separate them. You may enjoy using the sticky note technique I mentioned above, or a mind map approach that you can deploy online or on a whiteboard. You'll get the hang of basic mind mapping very quickly. Or you may thrive by talking through and notating the brain dump with a trusted colleague over lunch or over a beer after work.

3. **Note your direct experiences that relate to your main topic.** How can you shape your experiences to support the change you will be asking your audience to make? If you are speaking on health, what health issues have you overcome? If you are trying to get a school board to change a policy, what experiences did your child have with the current policy?

4. **Gather the direct data, either anecdotal or scientific, that support your topic.** Do preliminary searches for the kinds of data you think are relevant and that you believe will be credible. Please observe a simple and smart rule of research: tap the most respected and credible sources that are heavily used by journalists and academics first, and ignore a lot of the less authoritative research you'll find on Google searches.

5. **Identify any holes or vulnerabilities of logic or persuasiveness in your content.** What arguments could your audience present in response? How can you skillfully address those arguments? Identify the various objections that people might make to your theories, experience, or personality.

6. **Let the editing process begin.** Good content creation tends to be messy for a while, just like rehearsal. Don't get discouraged if you need more than a few drafts. You will. That's how writing works. Writing *is* rewriting. I suggest one of

the following approaches to editing: Go through your notes and choose the pieces, stories, and data that best serve the through-line (the connecting theme or plot in a movie, play, book, or speech) and the journey. Or choose what *not* to include, removing anything and everything that doesn't serve the through-line or advance the big idea and what you want your audience to think, feel, or do. This then becomes a recurring process: brain dump, organize, edit. However, remember this is also a creative experience: it's about what you like in a work process, and if you find a different system works better for you, great. Use this as a good starting place.

7. **Cut, cut, cut!** As you get to the later stages of the editing process, it's time to "murder your darlings." (Incidentally, despite years of misattribution, that phrase was first coined by Sir Arthur Quiller-Couch in his 1916 book *On the Art of Writing*.) Why is it so often offered as advice to writers? Because many of us tend to add more details and examples for important points to be sure the audience "gets it" or because we want them to think we're smart and know what we're talking about. Be careful of extraneous detail that disrupts the flow (such as the bit of historical context I offered above). Cut to the meat: choose the strongest detail or example or data point at critical parts of your story. Your audience often needs a lot less information to get to the "Aha!" moment than you might think.

Build In Contrast

During the next stage of the protocol you'll learn to build in *contrast*. This strategy makes a huge difference in performances. It's something that playwrights, directors, actors, composers, musicians, photographers, and so many other artists have mastered. It's not a new concept — although it may be new to you — it's the secret weapon for producing creative and compelling content and wowing an audience with your performance. I discovered it while in graduate school at NYU and it opened my eyes to what makes some performers fly high and others fall flat.

The purpose of using contrast when performing is simple and profound: to keep your audience engaged. Contrast is about intentionally building difference into your performances. It's about doing the unexpected, and it keeps audiences on their toes. We know attention spans and expectations are shaped by all of the entertainment we see, produced by the true masters of dramatic contrast at work in television, movies, and drama. Monotony bores your audience.

No one chooses to be monotonous; many of us come to know and like our own material so well that we lose perspective about how an audience will respond. Unless you use contrast as an intentional strategy, you run the risk of falling flat.

So, as you see the shape of your writing or content creation coming together on your wall, whiteboard, or laptop, you're going to look for areas to build in contrast of three different kinds:

1. *Structural Contrast:* how you organize the material and use types of content. It's about how you use stories, data, connecting narrative, and recommendations.

2. *Emotional Contrast:* how an audience experiences your performance emotionally. It's about how to strike different emotional notes — serious, moving, hopeful, sad, sardonic.

3. *Delivery Contrast:* how you deliver the content physically, orally, and visually. It's about how you vary your vocal pitch, tone, timing, and pacing and change up your visual elements and the speed of your movement on the stage and surrounding areas, whether platform, conference room, or classroom.

Many choices you make will involve more than one type of contrast, but let's look at them one at a time.

STRUCTURAL CONTRAST

Think about structural contrast in terms of how you arrange the elements of your content. Look for a rhythm as you weave together various threads of content. Say you're giving a speech at a sales conference. Your passage about sales trends and statistics flows into a story about a sales rep in the field and a lesson she learned from a client that is then broken up by a joke, before a transition into a major point about your department's future direction.

Any State of the Union speech can be studied for structural contrast as it balances these elements: statistic-example-policy prescription-inspirational story. Please remember the value of structural contrast for any performance. When you are being interviewed for a job, the judicious use of data, examples, stories, and details in presenting your qualifications will have a very favorable impact. The same applies to pitching a new business concept to an executive team.

I love the structural contrast from, yes, performers. For example, President Bill Clinton, in his 2012 Democratic National Convention address, moved so adeptly from telling facts (what he called "just arithmetic") to personal reflections to stories and political rhetoric. Oprah Winfrey's aforementioned commencement address at Stanford University in 2008 juxtaposed personal stories and confessions with life lessons, quotations, and a touch or two of data, all reinforcing her big idea that values and intuition form your strongest compass for success.

EMOTIONAL CONTRAST

Ideally, you'll take the audience on an emotional roller-coaster ride with you. The length, pitch, and drama of that ride will be determined, in part, by the type of speech you're giving and the kind of audience in the house. If you're giving a presentation to an audience of CFOs about a new approach to managing and presenting profit and loss data, you may not have geopolitical issues to contend with but you can still have momentous and moving moments. You can still use emotional contrast through humor with a good joke about accountants, by dramatizing the importance of their work to the economy with quotes and statistics, and by telling stories that stir their pride in their work.

Vice President Joe Biden is a master of emotional contrast in his public performances; his ability and willingness to shift emotional tones is pretty remarkable. He can be your slightly wacky but loving uncle at the swearing-in of new senators; the angry and stern COO of the free world, vowing retribution against ISIS; and the Frank Sinatra charmer on the campaign trail. In short, he knows how to reach his audience.

DELIVERY CONTRAST

I will delve into the planning, blocking, and execution of delivery contrast in more detail in future chapters as this involves your live performance in the spotlight. It's important to understand it conceptually first because you will begin to see how often you can use contrast to your advantage. You can create delivery contrast when you're performing by changing how you move in space, how you use visuals and auditory elements — your voice, of course, but also simple sound effects or music.

We experience and deal with delivery contrast every day. In a relaxed conversation with a friend, our language and vocal quality effortlessly move from storytelling to laughter to must-hear details to conspiratorial whispers. Our holiday offerings at Christmas and Hanukah are staged with lights, symbols, songs, and ritual. When we want to win key points in a meeting, we might show contrast by standing up and using the front of the conference room and whiteboard.

My business partner, Amy, pairs up with me for our Heroic Public Speaking Seminars, and I know that one of the reasons we're successful as a team is that we have great delivery contrast. I wear black; she wears white. She has great hair; I have no hair. My vocal quality is fast, staccato; hers is melodious and measured. I'm often described as fierce but gentle. She's often described as loving but firm. As business partners, co-presenters, and co-teachers, she's the performance *yin* to my *yang*. It's one of the reasons I originally asked her to join my company.

Here's a quick look at how you might introduce contrasts in developing important presentations that you deliver regularly or even daily at work.

To continue with the example above, let's say you're giving a speech about a new financial management software platform to an audience of two hundred auditors and accountants. Your big idea is that the new platform will equip them to educate managers about financial analysis and metrics with powerful communications and presentation tools, resulting in better numbers and margins. You introduce structural contrast by opening with a funny and interesting story about your grandfather's ledgers and the nature of accounting work before the rise of advanced computers. Then you transition cleanly to an all-business three-point analysis of your in-house study that found that corporate managers need to become better stewards of their numbers. You pause, and start building up the excitement and hope by describing how much easier it would be for the analysts to work with the line managers under the new system.

You paint in detail about each of the three major points, and then you pick three groups in the audience and assign them as the study group for each of the three points. When that point is mentioned in the speech, you ask that particular group to make a specific and clearly articulated point about the benefits of this method. Now you've added delivery contrast.

I can tell you what to do to be a remarkable performer, but in a book I cannot, of course, comment on your actual delivery. Knowing what to do to be a better performer is one big part of your learning process. You're getting that here. The other equally important part is the way you perform. If you need help with that, come find us at HeroicPublicSpeaking.com. We'll help you stop speaking and start performing.

SPEED REVIEW

Whether you're a number cruncher, a professional speaker looking to step up your game, or somewhere between those extremes, I'm confident that this chapter left you more capable of crafting the content that leads to the speeches, interviews, pitches, and performances that steal the show. Let's review the top points in the chapter:

1. Do a "get ready" exercise in order to begin the prep work for every presentation.

2. The first key to developing your content is to identify your big idea and related promise.

3. Once you have focused the big idea, the whole journey is about how you get your audience to consider and engage with that idea.

4. Your big idea should reflect what matters most to you; it should contain a promise and have personal and universal qualities.

5. You need to be able to describe the big idea succinctly and illustrate the costs of not changing and the rewards of being willing to embrace change.

6. Frameworks for developing your big idea into a speech include numerical, chronological, modular, compare and contrast, the three-act structure, and problem/solution.

7. Speeches typically fall into curriculum or message types, or a blend of the two.

8. Always incorporate emotional, structural, and delivery contrast into your content and performances.

9. A strong editing process uses the brain dump, organize, edit; brain dump, organize, edit rhythm.

10. Find a writing structure that works for you.

How to Create and Tell Stories That Make 'Em Laugh or Cry

WOULD YOU LIKE TO HAVE THE ABILITY to develop and tell the well-crafted story and effortlessly deliver a joke that people love? Would you like to be comfortable doing so in any setting, from your team's weekly meeting to a keynote speech? In this chapter, I'll show you how to get there in a way that is authentic to you and your personality. You may be intimidated by telling stories or jokes, but since stories and humor are applicable to virtually any life or business situation and are universal in their appeal, press the mute button on your inner critic and put aside any self-doubt that may try to get in your way.

The power of story gets a lot of attention, and why not? In fact, Amy Cosper, the editor in chief of *Entrepreneur* magazine, dubbed 2014 as the Year of the Story.[1] As discussed earlier, stories are marbled into our brains from the youngest age and are an ancient tradition of human expression. Cosper praises the virtue of storytelling in business, "Of all the highs and lows, storytelling seemed to be the major business lesson of 2014. Financials still matter to investors, but *your* story is now *the* story — and the one that will land you cash money." So, you see, hundreds of experts extol the importance of storytelling. I don't know how many times I've seen articles about how public speakers need to know how to tell stories. Well, telling stories is one thing; telling *good* stories is another endeavor altogether.

You may also be familiar with the advice that a presentation should begin with a story. But here's the truth: if you are opening with a story, it had better be a *great* story. Otherwise, open with a note that's intellectually or philosophically important. Often, when a speaker starts with a story, many in the audience think, *Oh, boy, here comes another one of those dull opening stories.* What's nonnegotiable is that your presentation needs to start with a moment that helps you connect with your audience.

Many people ask me how to find good stories without borrowing them from the Internet or friends. Sourcing and compiling stories is a valuable practice. Don't limit your story exploration to the high-pressure time you're preparing for a performance. You can discover story ideas and start refining them for later use by talking with friends and family members in a free-associative way that will spark ideas for you. It's a technique that I learned during my improv days, and you can use it too. Prospect for story ideas in sources such as:

- *People* — first friends, teachers you admired, your college roommate, your first girlfriend;

- *Places* — childhood summer camp or local hideout, a favorite family vacation spot, a relative's house you enjoyed visiting, first apartment you lived in when you were married;

- *Things* — your favorite baseball glove, your diary from your teen years, a fishing rod, a sweater your grandmother knitted for you, the ill-fitting suit your dad gave you that you wore at your first job;

- *Times/events* – a car accident, the first day of middle school, your daughter's confirmation, the day you dropped your first child off at college, an illness.

THE ELEMENTS OF THE SPOKEN STORY

As you begin thinking about and writing up potential stories, it's time to incorporate the elements of what makes good stories for public speaking and performance. You may have heard that it's important for stories to have a beginning, middle, and end. That's like telling me it's important to kick a soccer ball with a foot and five toes. A story may have a beginning, middle, and end, but knowing that doesn't necessarily help you tell a better story.

Let's go deeper using this five-step process for telling terrific tales.

1. **Choose stories that demonstrate the philosophical or practical application of your promise.** You'll find events when you can stretch to fit in a story you really like, but if you're speaking regularly to the same audience, they'll be turned off when they realize you're using your standard story over and over. However, if you're speaking to new audiences, why fix something that isn't broken?

2. **Communicate a passion and urgency for the story and a need to deliver it.** You may have heard one person tell a story to little effect, while another can make the same story work because he loves it and invests it with lots of energy and contrast.

3. **Raise the stakes as you're refining your story using the three-act structure.** Is your setup vivid and simple? Is your conflict told with enough detail and timing? Is your resolution as short as possible?

4. **Sculpt the story to serve the through-line.** Consider how to shape the story to support the changes you are asking the audience to make or the point you're trying to get across. If possible, I advise using stories from your own life — then it's fair to embellish and dramatize a few details to make your point. But stories about others can be just as effective.

5. **Use the three-act structure in writing and telling stories.** Act one: identify the given circumstances, the setting, time, people, and place. Act two: amplify the conflict, a challenge, struggle, different values, and different goals. Act three: reveal the resolution, a change, progress, or transformation.

Let's dig a little farther into the three-act structure because it's likely the most helpful storytelling structure. I've demonstrated how you can use the three-act structure for an entire speech, but each story within the speech can also use the three-act structure. For example, let's say I was telling a story about meeting my fiancée's parents. (By the way, this is a completely fabricated story. A fake. It didn't actually happen. I don't drink wine, I was never engaged to a woman named Mimi, and I don't bake pies.)

Act One: The given circumstances. Setting, time, people, and place. My hopes and objectives.

Mimi's family is very close ... much closer than I am with mine. They still live in the same house where she grew up, and I couldn't wait to see her old treehouse and sit out on the roof when everyone else was asleep. The first time we met was for Thanksgiving. I made a pie, my secret recipe. She had promised her parents would love me. I was going to prove to them that I was perfect. They would say, "How did we ever survive without Michael?"

Act Two:
The conflict. A struggle. Obstacles in the way.

Everything went wrong. I dropped the pie … the dog ate it. The dog then got sick. We drove the dog to the vet while the turkey was burning in the oven. The dog turned out to be allergic to my secret ingredient — coconut. And then I got us into a car accident with her parents' car. No one was hurt, thank God. But all the food was cold by the time we got back and no one had eaten a thing. We had to have hamburgers for Thanksgiving. The whole time, I just thought about how I had let Mimi down. I knew this would be our first and last holiday together. I was sneaking another glass of wine in the kitchen when I heard Mimi and her mom talking in hushed tones. I snuck over to the door so I could listen. She wanted us to go. She wanted me to go. I understood why. This was not the picture-perfect holiday they had envisioned.

Act Three:
The resolution. A change. Progress.
A transformation.

But you know what Mimi said? "This has been my favorite holiday ever, because all the people I love are here together. Give Michael another chance. Give Michael a hundred more chances. Maybe he's not perfect but he's perfect for me." There have been four more Thanksgivings, and each time something has gone wrong. But now it feels like home. It's better than perfect. It's ours.

Exercise:

Use one of the stories you discovered by thinking about people, places, things, or times/events and begin to flesh it out using the three-act structure: situation, conflict, resolution.

MAKE 'EM LAUGH

It's often recommended that you open a speech with a joke. Why? Obviously, it's great to get your audience laughing right off the bat. Give people a genuine laugh and you've put them at ease and made a quick connection. However, you're probably not a professional comedian. That's not your job. Telling a joke that doesn't land can let the wind out of your sails pretty quickly. So, if you don't want to tell jokes, don't. You can still get people to think differently, feel differently, and do what you want them to do. You can inspire them. You can thrill them. You can move them. All without ever telling a joke.

However, humor is the spice of life: a little here or there goes a long way. Also, it's a gift that keeps giving: when an audience laughs, they settle in to enjoy themselves and you loosen up and gain confidence to deliver your best. So, even though I'm not suggesting you hit the standup comedy circuit, there are some simple joke-telling tricks that will have them rolling in the aisles or at least wearing a genuine smile. (And, if you have any desire to be a *professional* speaker, you'll make a lot more money if you can make people laugh.)

And, let's be honest, who wouldn't love to be able to make people laugh? It really is a fantastic feeling to get people giggling. Their faces brighten up and their demeanor lightens up. Interestingly, I've found that the biggest laughs in a speech often come from improvised moments. Just recently, I delivered a *Book Yourself Solid* keynote for Transamerica, one of the country's largest financial services firms. Prior to my speech, there was a panel discussion on compliance issues about texting with clients. Apparently, it's a big no-no. So, of course, what did I do? I opened my speech by saying, "My advice to you: send texts to your clients." On paper, it's not particularly funny. But in the moment it killed. It broke the tension that had built up in the room over this issue. The audience roared with laughter.

I took a bow and said, "Thank you very much for having me. Good night!" and walked offstage. I came back ten seconds later.

So, if you'd like to try your hand at preparing a joke in advance or just want to learn how to find humor in the moment, here are eleven insights that will help you.

1. **A joke is often told in three acts.** If you know how to tell a story, then you know how to tell a joke. Most jokes are told like stories. They include exposition, conflict, and a resolution. Suspense is the key.

2. **Some jokes are told by putting together the completely unexpected, as in the two-story joke.** Story one leads down one path. Story two takes you down an alternate path that leads somewhere totally unexpected. Story one is the setup and story two is the punch line. Here's an example from Mel Brooks on the difference between tragedy and comedy:

   Story one: *Tragedy is when I cut my finger.*
   Story two: *Comedy is when you fall in an open sewer
      and die.*

   Notice that story one piques your interest because it's an obvious setup; cutting one's finger is not actually a tragedy. Your audience tries to guess where you're heading. Then comes story two, the punch line, with a twist where you give them something they don't expect. It's a delightful surprise. Just make sure they can't predict where you're going. If they can, the joke will fall flat.

   So how do you go about writing a joke? Here are two exercises to get you started:

   Write a provocative or interesting story one. Next, write down where your audience will *think* you're headed — their expectations. Then write story two and go in the opposite direction. For example:

> Story one: *A priest, a doctor, and a rabbi walk into a bar.*
> Story two: *The bartender says, "What is this, some kind of joke?"*

Or, a better one by Wendy Liebman; notice how the setup causes you to *expect* something.

> Story one: *The only way to really have safe sex is to abstain . . .*
> Story two: *. . . from drinking.*

The punch line delivers something different than expected. It reveals a *surprise*.

Exercise:

Record Jimmy Fallon or any other late-night program host doing a monologue. Hit pause on your remote just before the punch line. What do you think the punch line will be? Hit play to see what he actually says. Next step: write a better punch line. Good luck with that.

3. **Shared social context allows for instant recognition, thus the setup is achieved.** A lengthy explanation that would damage the joke or give a hint at the punch line isn't needed. This explains why so many jokes have the same setup: "Three men go into a bar." It's instantly recognized as a joke.

4. **Make the punch line *worth* the time they spent listening.** Craft a list of punch lines and try them out on friends, family, or a colleague. Professional comedians test and tweak their

jokes for months before finalizing them and using them in a club.

5. **Use the *rule of three* as a joke structure.** For example: same, same, different, such as a T-shirt that says PARIS, TOKYO, FARGO. Or, expected, expected, unexpected: *She was pretty . . . She was shapely . . . She was a man.*

    Professional comedians use the rule of three all the time. Chris Rock: *There are only three things women need in life: water, food, and compliments.* Jon Stewart: *I celebrated Thanksgiving in an old-fashioned way. I invited everyone in my neighborhood to my house. We had an enormous feast. Then I killed them all and took their land.* George Carlin: *One tequila, two tequila, three tequila, floor.*

6. **Laugh at yourself.** When you joke at your own expense, you defy expectations. The audience expects you to play to them with authority, but then you take them off-guard when your punch line points at you. A friend of mine was a speechwriter for a governor who became very unpopular but succeeded in rebuilding his support. Nonetheless, audiences were quite aware of his controversial record, and the governor would put them at ease with a couple lines that always got a laugh: "It's nice that people are waving at me with all five fingers now!" and, "When I was a kid my dad got me a summer job shoveling out the horse stables at the local track. I didn't know then it would be such a good apprenticeship for being governor."

7. **Don't tell everyone how funny your joke is going to be before you tell it.** If you do, the audience will sit back, cross their arms, and think, *Oh, yeah? Prove it. Let's see what you got, kid.* The best jokes are often the ones that sneak up and surprise your audience.

8. **Once you start, don't stop.** Commit to the joke or you won't get a laugh. If you back off as you're telling it or you tell it halfheartedly, the audience will feel your hesitation and assume the joke isn't going to be good. Also, avoid detours. Jokes usually work best in a straight line.

9. **Don't forget timing.** This is important to prepare and all the more important to execute. Timing requires real awareness on your part. You need to make sure that you deliver the punch line at the optimal moment. Part of that is keeping an eye on the room and your audience. Who's unsettled or restless? Do you have an interrupter in your midst? If there is a sudden distraction in the room or a lot of movement in one part of the audience, slow it down. Draw out the setup or the conflict so that the room is settled in time for your punch line.

10. **Create tension.** The optimal moment for the punch line is after you have built up tension with your setup. Take your time. Make them lean forward in their chairs. Then, when you deliver it, the tension will release with a bigger laugh. And what happens just before you deliver the punch line? *The pause* . . . of course. For timing, the biggest weapon in your arsenal is the pause. Don't rush it as you bring it home: "And the moral of the story is . . . [wait . . . wait . . . wait . . . then land it]." Also: a good joke gives the context quickly and efficiently, so the audience instantly recognizes the setup. If you take too long establishing the context, you're going to lose them.

11. **Be appropriate.** Be very, very careful of offensive and off-color humor. Know this: Bad humor selects weak targets. Great humor at someone's expense should only take on the most powerful folks in the room. That's the power dynamic of good comedy: if you're going to make a joke at someone's

expense, make a joke about someone who is in a higher position than most of the audience. You can make fun of the president or a well-known politico as long as it's not overtly political because that activates everybody's baggage. Jimmy Fallon made endless hay out of the buggy website for Obamacare but never let his Obama jokes get nasty or controversial. A little joke focused on the CEO of the company where you're speaking can put you on the side of the employees, and in most cases, the boss will take it just fine. Just be careful, and do your homework in advance.

While doing advance research to prepare for a corporate client, I discovered that the two guys running the company made for a great visual contrast — the president was as bald as I am, while the CEO had a gorgeous mane of well-groomed black hair. In doing my research, I checked around and not only heard that folks teased him about his manicured mane but I made sure he'd be okay if I poked a little fun at it.

So, the day of the speech arrived. A few weeks prior I had been given a T-shirt that says — WITH THIS BODY, WHO NEEDS HAIR? I thought it was hysterical, so I bought another one and brought it with me. The first thing I did after I was introduced by the CEO with the great hair was to make a big deal about his absolutely extraordinary shiny mane, how long it must take him to get it looking like that every day and how I'd kill for a head of hair like his. Then I asked the bald president to come up on the stage. Once I had him standing next to me, I told him that guys like us have to stick together, and I gave him the T-shirt (I had notified the video crew ahead of time so they could get a close-up shot of the shirt that could be read on the six giant screens in the convention center). It killed! Everybody loved it. You can get on the audience's side by needling the boss without going too far.

SO, A SKELETON WALKS INTO A BAR . . .

Let's review the key techniques for telling great stories and killing with your jokes:

- Source your stories through the people, places, events, and powerful objects of your own life.

- Raise the stakes and use the three-act structure.

- Shape your stories to support the changes you are asking your audience to make (use this in meetings and pitches too).

- For humor, work on jokes using the three-act structure or start the story one way, then reverse course to take the audience by surprise; leverage the rule of three; always aim barbed humor at yourself or the powerful people in the room (after you've done your homework); never be offensive; use shared context; and practice timing so you will own the room.

Oh, I almost forgot . . . a skeleton pulls up a barstool and motions with a bony finger – "Bartender, get me a cold beer . . . and a mop."

Now, that, my friend, is a terrible joke.

How to Rehearse and Stage
World-Class Performances

WHEN I STARTED SPEAKING PROFESSIONALLY, I already had five years of experience running meetings for hundreds of employees at a time; five years of experience as a professional actor; three years at NYU's Graduate Acting Program, where I earned my M.F.A. under the tutelage of some highly esteemed instructors; and another few years in college where I majored in theater. That translated into thousands of hours of studying and training in voice, speech, acting, singing, movement, body awareness, dramaturgy, directing, and more. When I began speaking professionally, I could pull it off because, in addition to my training as an actor and performer, I also learned how to produce content, I am pretty quick on my feet, and I can usually make people laugh.

But pulling it off is different from deserving, earning, and owning the stage. I wasn't masterful because I hadn't yet put in the hours to learn the discipline of public speaking. I did not connect that the time it takes to develop and rehearse a world-class theatrical production equated to delivering a speech or a similarly high-stakes performance.

But I do now. If you want to steal the show and create a meaningful experience for your audience, and if you want to truly own your career's spotlight moments, I hope you'll prepare differently than you've likely done in the past. This means rehearsing in a way that leaves as little to chance for your big moment as possible. Just to give you an idea, I spent roughly four hundred hours over five months preparing for my *Think Big Revolution* keynote. By preparing I mean I wrote, content mapped, used blocking techniques, directed, produced audio and visual elements, used improv methods to continue to develop and improve the content, memorized the material, rehearsed onstage, and received feedback from invited audiences. But remember, it's not just putting in the requisite time and effort, it's *how* you rehearse that matters. With this said, I don't expect you to spend nearly this much time on rehearsal unless you make your living giving speeches. I share this extreme example with you to demonstrate the amount of time that goes into creating world-class performances. I'm simply suggesting that you consider dedicating more time to your preparation.

Let's get this out of the way first: What expectations do you have about rehearsing for your presentation or performance? How do you approach rehearsal now? Do you think about your speech in your head, or do you rehearse on your feet, out loud? Do you learn everything you can about the facility or room where you'll be presenting at the earliest possible moment, or do you show up on the day and hope that what you've created will work? Do you rehearse in front of a mirror?

By the way, the rehearsing-in-front-of-the-mirror thing is as odd as the "imagine your audience naked" advice. How does looking at oneself while performing make any sense? How are you supposed to react to a mirror image of your face? Find me one award-winning actor who rehearses in front of a mirror and I'll eat my words. The only time you'll see a professional looking in the mirror is either (A) to experiment with facial prosthetics or makeup and costume to alter their looks or (B) to admire their jawline. In fact, you'll probably see the latter more often than the former.

THE SEVEN STEPS TO SUCCESSFUL REHEARSALS THAT PRODUCE GREAT PERFORMANCES

Why Should You Rehearse?

Tell me if this seems like a crazy idea: giving a live speech onstage in front of an audience and barely rehearsing beforehand.

I'll let you in on a secret: it happens all the time. Okay, maybe you've done it. But does it really make any sense at all? Even a priest or rabbi (or choose your equivalent celebrant) makes you rehearse for your wedding ceremony, yet most people resist it and find it nerve-wracking.

The importance of holding effective rehearsals and knowing what makes them effective is the most commonly misunderstood area among the people we coach. It is also the biggest gap between a trained performer and a person who doesn't do a lot of public speaking. If you aren't well rehearsed, you've stacked the odds against giving the performance you want to give. My goal in this chapter is to turn those odds around.

Here's what I typically see: Most people procrastinate to some degree and spend very little time rehearsing for an important moment — a job interview, a speech, or a meeting. If they do rehearse, they do so in their heads or in their living room for a few minutes at a time. The truth is most people wing it – I know, because I've done it myself.

The results are common mistakes: changing the content at the last minute; focusing too much on visuals rather than on content and performance; relying too much on notes; thinking that you don't need to rehearse the stories you're going to tell because they're moments you've lived. I also frequently hear something along these lines: "I find rehearsing makes me nervous so I keep it to a minimum." That's even more of a reason to rehearse – to keep your nerves at bay for your big moment.

This brings me to another point, if anxiety or nerves are part of why you are here with me. Going through the steps for an effective rehearsal will help you master the inner game of performance by redirecting your mental focus. You often psych yourself out worrying *about* the speech rather than working on it. You may obsess over how you're going to perform, who is going to be in the audience, how you'll be received and perceived, and how you should prepare for it. This continues to feed your stress, which sets you up for more avoidance behaviors rather than moving you forward. This way, you keep adding to your anxiety rather than creating confidence. Moreover, the best way to reduce anxiety is to actually know *what* you're doing and *how* you're going to do it.

It may seem obvious, but the fact is our brains work this way. If you go through the rehearsal process effectively, you deepen the grooves in your mind around the words you're memorizing, the movements you're blocking, and the emotional connection you're making to your material so you can confidently deliver your presentation with less self-consciousness. By creating these new neural pathways and connections, you're helping your brain so it doesn't have to work as hard to do all the things you want it to do when you perform. You're creating new muscle memories you can access effortlessly with unconscious competence. The rehearsal process builds one very thin layer of experience at a time, strengthening those pathways every time you work through your material. This is an important part in the process, so keep it in mind.

Maybe you're an experienced speaker. Maybe you already make a commitment to prepare. That's fantastic. The reality of performing in the spotlight – whether it's a conference room for an interview or an auditorium stage at Davos – is that no matter how much you've prepared, no matter how confident you are, even if you're an experienced speaker, the audience will only know and remember what you give them *live*. You don't get points from your audience for the show you rehearsed in your hotel room. That's the difference between the spotlight and the screen: *you can't edit the show one last time while you're performing it*. My rehearsal process gives you a reliable approach for translating the performance you effectively *prepare* into the performance you *deliver* – but it still allows for spontaneity and improvisation.

In Chapter 10, you worked on and polished *what* you're going to say: your big idea, your promise, and more. Rehearsal is where you explore, prepare, and internalize *how* you're going to perform; it's where you work on *showing* the audience your big idea, not just *telling* them about it. My seven-step process for successful rehearsals that turn into great performances will make this transition accessible and even fun (that's when you'll know you're making progress – when you're having fun). The seven steps are:

1. Table reads

2. Content mapping

3. Blocking (I'll also address props, costumes, and use of multimedia)

4. Improvisation and rewriting

5. Invited rehearsal (maybe even with a coach or peer with actual training)

6. Open rehearsal (with people in your target audience)

7. Dress/tech rehearsal

During this discussion, I'll also provide tips and techniques for universal concerns such as wardrobe, memorization, and the unbeatable strategy for when and how to use slides and other visual aids.

Step 1: Table Reads

Okay, you've got your speech, talking points, script, or other form of content. The first step, which I've adopted from theater and screen, is the *table read*. A table read is when actors sit around tables in a large room and read through the script out loud. This lets the actors make sense of the material, and it allows the writers and the creative team to hear how the script sounds. So, a table read serves a number of good purposes. The actors don't attempt Academy Award–winning performances at the table read; rather, they simply try to get a feel for the story, the relationships between characters, rhythm, pacing of the language, and more. They try to make sense of the story.

Now you try it. Sit in a quiet space (at the dining room table will work just fine) with good seating and lighting and read your content aloud. You can do a table read with a trusted mentor or friend who will listen and provide only high-level general impressions. You can also table read alone, perhaps making an audio recording for playback and review on your smart phone.

I want you to sit and read for a few reasons.

1. Reading aloud lowers expectations and allows you to start working on the material by easing into it.

2. By sitting, you take away any distraction of your body and stage movements so you can focus on the words and how they sound and feel when you let them leave your mind to be spoken aloud. There's a big difference. You don't have to think about gestures, eye contact, or blocking.

3. By keeping your eyes on the page, it's easier to absorb the words, their rhythm, and their feel (yes, words have feeling; *cut* feels different than *love* when you say them out loud). Table reads work for an outlined speech as well as for a formally written speech; simply incorporate the spoken material you'll be using between the big scripted points in your outline.

4. Remember, writing content and saying it out loud are very different, and this is where you can begin to explore the friction between the two. For example, writers can make use of punctuation, headings, layout, and other graphic/visual effects in written text. A speaker can use timing, tone, volume, and timbre to add emotional context. It's also possible to leave much unsaid or implied when speaking directly to a few people or even a large audience.

Table reads can take place over a few days or more. After each reading, make general notes on passages you will want to revisit and think about later in the process. Additionally, written language and spoken language often have different rhythms, paces, and styles. The table read is where you begin to turn your written language into spoken language. However, when you write a speech, try to write in the way that you speak, not in the way your eighth-grade English teacher taught you to write. Most of all, this gets you ready to do content mapping in Step 2.

Step 2: Content Mapping

After a few table reads, you're ready to start mapping your written material for a live rehearsal. You'll do this by marking up the printed pages with notes on how you want to deliver your spoken words: sounds, pace, emphasis, and more.

Content mapping allows you to work deeper into the experience of your presentation as you speak it. You will learn what makes certain passages sing and others fall flat. You will discover the poetic words and phrases in your material as well as the run-on sentences. You will see how to tighten up your opening story or add an extra pause to the punch line you're going to land.

Your goal is to arrive at a map of the vocal presentation of your speech. The words you emphasize, and the words you throw away. The pauses you want to use every time.

Yes, many things will change from performance to performance, but by working through and sculpting the backbone of how you will deliver the words, you'll start wiring your brain for *performing* the content, not reading it. On page 126, you'll find a typeset re-creation of two paragraphs of my *Think Big Manifesto* speech that shows how I content mapped those pages, with the code I use for the shorthand.

The elements of your content map are:

- **Beats** – pauses, long and short, are moments that emphasize a point, turn into a transition, or allow for a listener to absorb an idea.

- **Operative words** – the most important words in the sentence to communicate the meaning, as you believe it to be. The ways to make a word operative include volume, pitch, tone, pauses, linking, extending a vowel, or sharpening a consonant. Note Kennedy's operative words in this sentence: "And yet the **same** revolutionary beliefs for which our **fore-bears fought** are still at issue around **the globe** – the **belief** that the rights of **man** come not from the **generosity** of the **state** but from the **hand of God**." *Same* is an operative word because it supports the major concept of the sentence.

Excerpt from the Think Big Revolution Keynote

Joseph Campbell once said,|| "The privilege,|| the privilege of a lifetime||is being who you are." Well, this is who I am. What I just told you,||what you see in front of you,||what's in my books,||they're all just parts of me.||I believed in this presentation for a long time. I have believed in thinking big for a long, long, long time. Long before I was able to do it,|| because I,||Michael Port, stand for thinking bigger about who you are and about what you offer the world.

Stand on chair

off chair downstage

See, I want to think bigger in my world, and I want to help you think bigger in yours. Everything I do in my work and my personal life is driven by this purpose. I decided to stop being big and actually start playing big instead.

go into house

Look,||I'm not going to stand up here and tell you that I know what thinking big looks like to you. I don't know what your dreams are. But I know that you have them. And I also know that I'm not somehow special. I'm not the only person that is willing to stand for something.

- **Lists** — the use of beats, emphasis, timing, and rhythm to deliver the elements of a list with the emphasis you want. In this list from Kennedy's 1961 inaugural address, note how he uses beats to give the list mounting power: "Let every nation know, whether it wishes us well or ill, that we shall pay any price, bear any burden, meet any hardship, support any friend, oppose any foe to assure the survival and the success of liberty." Additionally, if you listen to the speech, you'll notice how he builds tension with each successful bullet point. He drives through them toward the end of the points even though he puts a beat in between each point. That forward movement is compelling to listen to. He doesn't drop the energy with each successful point. Rather, he *increases* the importance of each point through to the end.

- **Parentheticals** — the vocal shift we make when we share an idea as if it is in parentheses.

- **Repetition** — the use of beats and emphasis to vocalize repeated words, such as my use of "long, long, long time" in my script on page 126.

- **Rhythm** — the pacing you use to vocalize one-syllable and multisyllable words in a sentence. Savor the texture and tension of how Kennedy delivers this long sentence with its purposeful weaving of short and longer words: "Now the **trumpet summons us again** — not as a call to bear arms, though arms we need — not as a **call to battle, though embattled we are** — but a **call to bear the burden of a long twilight struggle,** year in and year out, 'rejoicing in hope, patient in tribulation' — a struggle against the **common enemies of man: tyranny, poverty, disease and war itself.**"

In the mapping process, create as much vocal contrast as you can. Content mapping your text creates the foundation upon which you will stage your presentation. *This doesn't mean that you're constrained to deliver the language exactly as mapped when giving your speech.* Far from it, because as you integrate elements of improv when you are rehearsing, your content map may change.

If you're working from an outline rather than a complete text, you should still content map it because there will be passages and stories that you'll share as though they were scripted, employing the same punch line, same rhythms, and same operative words.

To learn more about content mapping, visit the free video training section at www.StealtheShow.com and you'll be able to look over my shoulder as I content map actual text from one of my speeches.

Now it's time to restart your table reads (out loud, always out loud) and content map your text.

Step 3: Blocking

Blocking is your plan for how you will move during your performance in varying degrees of detail depending upon your style, the space you're in, and the event itself. Most commencement speakers are expected to stay behind the podium, for example. But that doesn't mean you have to. For most speeches, if you can, try to avoid speaking from behind a podium (or any other piece of furniture, for that matter). A podium puts a barrier between you and the audience. People will often choose to stay behind a podium as a way of hiding from the audience or simply because they need to read their speech.

Remember the importance of contrast in your performances? If you're behind a podium for more than a few minutes, your physicality doesn't change. Your lack of movement offers only visual and kinesthetic sameness. With that said, also remember my mantra that there isn't one way to perform. Performance of all kinds is an art, and every situation and performer are different. There may be times when speaking from behind a podium is perfect, although the one time I tried it, I bombed. But, hey, that might just be me. Just like all the choices you make when performing, if you choose to stand behind a podium, make sure you're doing so for the right reasons. And practically, if it's a long speech and you need notes, you'll likely need the podium.

Blocking will involve considerations such as the use of props, costumes, and multimedia, as well as how you will choreograph your use of the specific performance space where you'll next deliver the presentation. This could be a conference room where you'll be having negotiations on a deal or, more commonly, a stage, hotel meeting room, or large auditorium. When your performance is fully blocked, the process of polishing and refinement begins as you deliver your lines using your notes while practicing movement.

In a speech that's not been blocked or rehearsed, you can see the telltale signs. Typically you'll see the speaker pacing; wandering around the stage; shifting his weight uncomfortably; displaying discomfort with his hands; hiding behind the podium or other props; repeating gestures; feeling trapped in one spot; continuously looking down at the ground or at the computer screen; standing too close to the audience or too far from them; or not finding the light and standing in the dark. These characteristics are indicative of someone who has not rehearsed her performance — whether she is on a stage or in a job interview.

It's important to learn blocking because it will solve most of these problems. In case you're interested, the term *blocking* comes from the practice of nineteenth-century theatre directors, who worked out the staging of a scene on a miniature stage using blocks to represent each of the actors.

When you block your movement, you're moving in a way that

enhances your message and creates dynamics through contrast. It actually also helps you remember your material because it anchors it in different parts of the stage, and you can continue to revisit that part of the stage when unpacking that content. Blocking also helps the audience understand and digest your content by creating a visual flow. I often have students ask me if blocking is too confining or overscripted for a presentation. There are two answers: One, as I've said, by polishing and perfecting your intentional movement plan through rehearsal, you develop the muscle memory and confidence to improvise. Two, blocking provides in most cases a richer, cleaner visual experience to help allow your big idea and all your content to land with power and purpose.

Start this step by making blocking notations in your script using macro and micro stage directions. Macro directions are:

- US – upstage
- DS – downstage
- SL – stage left
- SR – stage right

Micro directions are specific movements on specific words that can include but are not limited to:

- Sitting
- Kneeling
- Standing on a chair
- Going down into the house

Keep in mind some basic blocking no-nos:

- Don't spend too much time close to the front row if you are not on a stage because it will be harder for the audience in the back rows to see you. Plus, you don't really want the front row staring at your crotch, do you? Don't answer that.

- Don't spend too much time in one part of the stage, whether stage left or stage right, upstage or downstage: you want to use the stage to connect with *all* the seats.

- Don't present in the dark—"finding your light" is a theater term for making sure that you are always lit. You want the audience to see your bright smile and beautiful eyes, don't you? Hotel ballrooms are notoriously problematic when it comes to lighting. Examine how the stage or platform is lit (typically from above) as part of your preparation, and when you are presenting, keep in mind that you always want to find your light.

But here's the key: You have to know your material well enough so that even if you didn't do any of the blocking you rehearsed, you would still be fine. Stay flexible, even after content mapping and blocking your material. Why? Venues will be different. Lights will be different. Remain adaptable. Apply your blocking to your venue.

You might have heard that you shouldn't walk and talk at the same time onstage. That doesn't make sense—people do it all the time in real life, so why not on the stage as well? You want to be as authentic and natural as possible, don't you? I think the intended gist of this advice is that you shouldn't walk while speaking important statements or during key moments. That advice is right-on. Just remember that not everything you are saying is of equal importance. Movement is a good time for transitions, secondary points, or getting to the other side of the stage to answer a question. So, you can walk and talk at the same time but not while delivering the most important points. Block out what kind of content you can move on — and what is important to stand and land on. Let your punch lines, point lines, and purpose lines land.

On Doing More with Movement

Stage movement and the use of your body are major areas of technique that you can pursue to advance your skills. Actors work on these techniques for years and theirs is not a standard I'd ever expect you to meet. For our discussion here, I'll keep it simple. If you want to go further in working on movement and your body, I recommend finding a skilled coach/trainer (go to HeroicPublicSpeaking.com). This really might be of interest if you speak professionally or frequently, have to give important speeches a few times a year, or have a high-stakes presentation coming up soon.

What are you striving for in how you move and use your body? Movement work was something that made me stand out right off the bat — folks were used to the typical pacing and wandering, which makes weak content look even worse.

Let's start with the optimal posture for your work onstage. You want to be loose and unconstrained, don't you? If so, do a little exercise. Let your hands hang freely at your sides. With your shoulders aligned over your hips and your hips aligned over your ankles, take a deep breath that fills your lungs and expands your ribcage and then, on an exhale, let the tension flow out of your neck-arms-torso-legs-feet. Do this at least ten times. Your muscles will relax with each exhalation. You may even feel your energy increase as you soften your body. When you are relaxed and comfortable in your body, you feel like you can move easily and naturally in front of an audience. In doing so, you will feel more powerful, command attention, and own the room.

As part of your review during rehearsals, self-assess and note the microgestures that will be distracting to your audience and gradually work them out of your repertoire. Do you:

- Thrust your shoulders back military-style?

- Thrust your hips forward or to one side?

- Turn your feet out?

- Tend to lick your lips?

- Repeatedly flip or smooth your hair?

- Hike up your pants?

- Button and unbutton your blazer?

- Find your hands inadvertently wandering too close to the family jewels? (Unconsciously you might be protecting yourself because you feel exposed to strangers.)

Don't beat yourself up over any of these — especially guarding the family jewels. Just take note if they're happening and move on. Do the same after each rehearsal.

Costumes, Props, and Media

Moving into rehearsal is about moving through a continuum where you translate ideas and content into movement, voice, and performance. It's a continuum where you will be thinking more visually as you approach the final product of your presentation. That's why I'm introducing the use of costumes, props, and media in this step. These are all visual tools to get your message across and to make your performances more memorable.

Every time you make any public presentation or appearance, the clothes on your back are your costume. In television your clothes are called *wardrobe,* just as in the service business they're called a *uniform.* Your clothing choices for a public presentation of any kind are a representation of your message and brand in the eyes of your audience. They should amplify your personal brand, not distract people from your message.

Is what you wear really that important? Yes. You are playing a character when you perform, a character made up of your best and most useful attributes, and your clothing choices contribute to your character development. By thinking about costume, you're developing the useful skill of understanding how others see you. In most cases, you're still choosing from the narrow band of options available in the business casual to business formal range. I'm sure you can think of many examples of how individual performers find the costume that fits their brand while also being comfortable. Here are a few:

- Comic and actor Chris Rock in his standup performances — edgy, ruthlessly incisive comic speaking truth in variations on black pullover, black slacks, and black comfortable shoes, at times adding a casual black leather jacket. For higher-profile concert venues he may wear a fitted gray or black suit, only rarely with a tie.

- Business advisor, author, and all-around great guy Chris Brogan — gentle hipster digital media sage who is comfortable showing some New England nerd as well: basic jeans or chinos with a T-shirt and comfortable suit jacket, or a comfortable but quality striped button-down.

- Author, marketing and business-development genius, salt-of-the-earth kind of guy John Jantsch — shows midwestern authenticity in his blazer, jeans, and Converse high-tops. You'll rarely ever catch him in a suit and tie, yet he always looks clean-cut and classy.

- Speaker and high-level author for publications such as the *Harvard Business Review* and *Forbes* and one of the most likable people I know, Dorie Clark — looking strong, steady, and intellectual in slacks, blazers, preppy button-down shirts, and her hair cropped short.

- Social media author, major online brand, and most authentic and generous friend to many, Scott Stratten — a grungy, irreverent hipster with a long beard, out-of-control hair, and tattoo-covered arms. Nine times out of ten you'll find Stratten dressed in a black T-shirt and well-worn jeans. Yet he speaks at the biggest business conferences with audiences dressed to the nines in business attire.

- Amy, co-founder of HeroicPublicSpeaking.com — stylish, comfortable clothing. She never looks like she's trying too hard or wants to outshine anyone else. In fact, in some of the photos on our website, she's not even wearing shoes. She says she feels more grounded and it allows her to move more naturally. She looks warm and approachable; a beautiful representation of her brand, which is based on self-expression, power, and play.

- Consultant and bestselling author Daniel Pink — authoritative business guru and super-smart guy with the traditional costume of the approachable consultant: loose-fitting slacks, button-down shirt, and casual blazer, or casual suit with no tie and casual loafers.

You want to rehearse using your performance costume as early as possible so that you have experienced the effect of your costume on your ability to move and express yourself and because it is part of your character — especially the shoes. In choosing your wardrobe, both men and women should keep in mind that you don't want any aspect of your personal presentation to distract the audience from your spoken presentation.

POINTS OF EMPHASIS FOR MEN
WHEN CHOOSING CLOTHING:

- Do be consistent with brand.

- Do wear shoes with soles that grip and don't make much noise.

- Don't wear too-tight pants, pants that are hiked up too high, or clothes that reveal too much (unless, of course, your name is Adam Levine or Mick Jagger).

- Do pick out a blazer (if that's part of your costume) that gives you good range of movement – too tight in the shoulders won't allow you to lift your arms.

- Don't keep doing and undoing the button on your blazer, it gets distracting for viewers.

- Don't wear busy or clashing patterns – unless that's part of your personal brand.

- Don't wear colors like lavender, mint green, gray, or light blue if you sweat a lot; black or white shirts will hide the pit stains.

POINTS OF EMPHASIS FOR WOMEN
WHEN CHOOSING CLOTHING:

- Do be consistent with your brand.

- Don't wear clothes that reveal too much (unless that's part of your brand).

- Do consider whether a mic pack (a transmitter) and lavaliere (a little portable microphone that attaches to your shirt) will work with your outfit – will you be able to clip the lavaliere to your top without ruining the look? And do you have a belt or pocket you can attach the transmitter to?

- Don't wear noisy jewelry like bangles, bauble-heavy necklaces, or large hanging earrings that may be picked up by the microphone. Even if you're not wearing a mic, stay away from jewelry that makes noise because it can be distracting.

- Do be very careful about choosing spiky heels or very high heels. They can make a lot of noise when you walk and can inhibit movement — if the audience thinks you look uncomfortable, you'll look weak and you'll lose some of your power.

- Do keep your hair — if it is long — out of your face for sight lines and so that you won't constantly do the hair flip, which tends to drive audiences mad.

- Do notice how your skirt line changes when you're sitting down.

- Don't wear a short skirt if you're on a stage or platform that is higher than the audience because, well ... you understand why.

- Don't wear a short skirt if you think you'll keep pulling it down because it rides up your legs.

- Don't wear dresses that are too long because they may trip you, and even if they don't, if the audience thinks you might trip, it will make them uncomfortable and distract them from listening to you and your message.

- Do be mindful of how the light affects your clothing because some clothing, especially sheer pieces, can become see-through under the lights.

Props

Props can at times be more powerful to an audience than a verbal description. They have a unique power in being tangible objects that your audience can see and feel and, if appropriate, touch. Though be sure to ask yourself: is the prop truly useful to illustrate a point for the audience? If not, skip it. However, don't underestimate the potential of a prop for small group performances such as meetings or deal pitches. There are three ways to use a prop effectively:

1. To transform ordinary objects into make-believe things to demonstrate a concept or tell a story. For example, using a pen as a ruler to demonstrate how your third-grade teacher rapped on your knuckles when you spoke out in class, or as a chopstick to tell the story about meeting your wife at a restaurant in Chinatown, or as the knife that cut your finger when you were slicing bread.

2. To control timing, in the way that comedians sharpen suspense during a performance by using their bottle of water after a particular line takes off with the audience to let the moment ride for an extra beat or two.

3. To create an unforgettable image to illustrate a point in a way you can't by just telling it. A few examples: Jill Bolte Taylor uses an actual human brain during her TED talk about her massive stroke and the insights into life that she gained from it. The prop is effective because it gives the audience a visual, memorable sense of the basic structure of the brain, which is key to the rest of the talk. Vice President Al Gore made television history in 1993 during an appearance on *The David Letterman Show*. Gore was there to draw attention to his role in auditing wasteful spending in federal agencies — a painfully dry topic to explain. He demonstrated that the feds actually bother to test the shatter point of U.S. regulation "ash receivers" — glass ashtrays — by smashing an ashtray with a hammer on Letterman's desk. Bill Gates used a prop brilliantly during

his 2009 TED talk about eradicating malaria, a disease whose seriousness is overlooked by the West, when he surprised the audience by releasing a jarful of mosquitoes into the auditorium (he immediately said they weren't carrying malaria, something the audience needed to hear). One of my students, Beth Allen, brings a toilet onstage (yes, an actual porcelain toilet), among other props, because she teaches DIY home repairs for women. It works brilliantly.

OTHER CONSIDERATIONS FOR USING PROPS:

- They should be large enough to be seen easily in the room or auditorium where you're presenting.
- Once your speech is "on its feet" and well blocked, rehearse with your prop every time.
- If the prop is even partially mechanical or electronic, double-check that it is working before you go on.

Slide Decks and Other Media

Here's the typical question folks ask themselves about the use of projected slides to accompany a presentation, whether through PowerPoint, Keynote, or another slideware app: should I go with slides or without slides? But we can do better because to use slides or not to use slides is not the question.

Instead, I recommend asking: how can I use slides and other media in a unique way that will stir my audience emotionally or cement a major point with a strong visual? And expand your thinking beyond slides to consider video and audio. Only include slides or other media if your choices will be visually powerful, creating more contrast and providing the element of surprise with images or audio that are new to your audience.

Among some iconic presentations that meet these three standards: Check out Randy Pausch's last lecture, given at Carnegie Mellon University in 2007. The year before, Professor Pausch was given a diagnosis of terminal pancreatic cancer. In a powerful twist on a popular ongoing lecture series tradition where professors are asked to think deeply about what matters to them and give a no-holds-barred lecture summarizing their strongest arguments and views, Pausch gave what was pretty much the last lecture of his life, one that he aptly titled, "The Last Lecture: Really Achieving Your Childhood Dreams."

Pausch gave an upbeat, generous, and honest lecture (he was still healthy, did pushups onstage, used lots of humor, such as leading the talk saying he had experienced a deathbed conversion and bought a Macintosh computer) that became an Internet sensation and led to a book deal. His lecture uses a blend of text, video, and audio that illustrates his narrative, offers visual contrast, and delivers lots of delight and surprise through examples of his students' groundbreaking use of computer animation, among other things. Pausch passed away in 2008 but left several great legacies, including his last lecture.

There's another lesson in Pausch's speech. It wasn't technically perfect. He relied heavily on his notes and spent a fair amount of time referring to them, sometimes even reading from them. Yet because he was so open, honest, and vulnerable, and because he built in lots of contrast and offered an incredibly well-thought-out and organized speech, he connected with millions worldwide. I've mentioned this before but it bears repeating: Perfection is largely unattainable. It is often the enemy of good. I don't expect you to master every single piece of technical advice I share with you. Even changing or improving a few things or increasing your skills in a few areas can help you nail a performance with style and grace.

When I deliver my *Book Yourself Solid* keynote, I rarely use slides. One of the greatest compliments I've ever received was from someone who shared on Facebook that he thought Seth Godin and I were the two greatest speakers he'd seen: "Seth because of his ability to use more than 150 unique slides during a presentation and Michael Port because he can keep an audience on the edge of their seat for 90 minutes without using one slide." For the record, as much as I appreciate the sentiment, I don't believe it for a second. Knowing Seth, I'm sure I can speak for him as well when I say that we are *not* actually the two greatest speakers *in the world*. I only use this example to demonstrate that, once again, there isn't one right way to deliver a presentation.

In *The Think Big Revolution* keynote I use lots of different media, but not in the way that you might think. Before the section entitled "Stand for Something, or Someone Will Stand on You," I show a one-minute video that includes dozens of five-second clips of my students, each on their own in their homes, standing up, hands on hearts, declaring what they stand for. It's powerful and something that I ask my audience to do as well. I also show pictures of me as a husky kid during the section where I talk about my issues with food that track back to childhood. Additionally, I perform scenes where I talk to voices played through the speakers in the theater. It's a dynamic that audience members have likely never seen at another keynote and it creates a lot of contrast at a business conference, along with a compelling novelty factor. To see these examples and more, you can watch a short excerpt of the keynote at www.MichaelPort.com.

When Amy and I perform *Steal the Show, A Keynote in One Act,* we use both visuals and audio to help tell the story. Our keynote takes place on and off an airplane. Sometimes the visuals are simply black slides with white text to set up a location for a particular scene ("a coffee shop on Thursday") or to fast-forward time ("three years later"). We use the sound of an airplane seatbelt *ding* to represent transitions on and off the plane. We also show a one-minute video that I shot and edited of Amy as a little girl getting scolded by her mother. Amy's daughter, Ruby, plays Amy as a young child and Amy plays a fictitious version of her mother.

You're only limited by your imagination and what you think is expected. A few years ago, a conference organizer asked me when I was going to send in slides for my *Book Yourself Solid* keynote. I let her know that I didn't need them; however, she insisted I use them because "good presentations have slides." I was surprised. After all, she'd seen full-length videos of my keynote and had engaged me for the event, so she was familiar with my work and performance style. I took the time to talk to her about why I didn't need them for this presentation so that she'd understand and hopefully support my methodology. She did support me, I didn't use slides, and she subsequently hired me to present at numerous other events.

It's important to stand up for your work and style so that you can provide the best possible experience for your audience. If you've done the work and know what works, then stick with it. Don't change on a whim because someone has an unnecessary or unrealistic expectation of what you *should* do. Remember, speaking is performing and performing is an art and there isn't one way to make art. You're working toward a breakthrough performance that changes the world and your life; don't settle for anything less than your best. Trust yourself.

Keep these tips in mind when deciding to use PowerPoint or Keynote or other slideware:

- Don't use slides as cue cards — if you need your slides to remind you what to talk about next, more rehearsal is in order.

- Use slides that add to or reinforce what you say but do not repeat it or you risk making yourself redundant.

- Stay connected with the audience when you show slides (don't look at the screen unless it's a choice to make a point or highlight an idea or something else).

- Don't use stock images, or at least try to avoid them — you're using visuals to create a sense of time or place, create emotional connection, or add humor or contrast to your performance. Stock images are generally impersonal.

- If you do use slides, you don't need to point the remote at the screen. The screen doesn't actually advance your slides; that's the computer's job. Moreover, the remote broadcasts a wide signal so you don't usually need to point it at your computer either. Try to make the remote an extension of your hand rather than an object that you have to interact with to advance a slide.

Step 4: Improvisation

Improvisation is one of the most powerful secrets from the actor's trade that all successful people employ to some degree. Improv involves the ability to listen in the moment, trust your intuition, collaborate, accept and respond to feedback, revise, and rehearse or perform again. Improv works — and it's neat that by adding an "e" it becomes *improve,* because that's just what it does.

In *Steal the Show,* I'm addressing improv in two dimensions that are applicable to you: improv during a rehearsal, and improv during a performance to save difficult moments or to seize an opportunity for humor, fun, or a connection with your audience. In this step, I'm going to focus on the uses of improv during rehearsal and not address the entire subject, which is introduced in Chapter 7, where you read about the improv technique of *yes, and . . .* , and is covered in depth in Chapter 14.

During rehearsal, improv is all about making choices about your content, blocking, and delivery. It's about trying on different objectives as you go through your script. You use improv during rehearsal as you're working through your script out loud, hearing the words. This is often where I see folks make big improvements in their content. Some of us, no matter how hard we try, still write the way we were taught to write, not so much the way we talk. In preparing for a speech, you're seeking to find your public voice as a performer. Improving the moments in your script that feel forced or stilted can yield gold.

Improv also perks up your blocking: as you try a movement that doesn't work, you improvise different ideas, find one you potentially like, and then revise and edit your blocking and content map. Then, do it again: improvise, rewrite, and improvise some more. You may be telling the same story for the umpteenth time during your rehearsals, but when a fresh detail comes out of an improvisation, it can click as the killer moment that makes your story really land.

There are two ways you can improvise your content:

1. Use **an outlined structure.** If following an outlined structure, make the materials work inside that outline. Then respond and perhaps even reorganize your material based on what's happening in the moment. This is why rehearsal and knowing your material well matter so much.

2. Use **a scripted structure.** If you decide on a scripted structure, you can still bring a spontaneous, improvisational feel to it. You can go off script, as long as you know when to pick it back up. Perform as though it's unscripted – the first time you've ever said it. It's the difference between feeling like

the content is fresh and spontaneous and feeling like you are plodding along and regurgitating the material.

Steps 5 and 6 — Invited Rehearsals and Open Rehearsals

At this point, you move into the crucial phase of live rehearsals. You can get better when you rehearse by yourself, certainly. But you can get exponentially better when you rehearse in front of others. **Step 5** to rehearsing successfully is the *invited rehearsal.* This is where you invite a select group who will serve as your audience and offer feedback. As you perform your invited rehearsal, keep in mind that this is not a run-through; you can always stop and start. I advise you to choose the key or troubling passages, perform them first, and ask for feedback.

Start holding invited rehearsals before your entire speech is ready. In fact, it shouldn't be ready, since you are still rehearsing and tweaking. Think about it this way: it's better to bring people in early than to write an entire speech and only then get feedback that it doesn't work. Even if there are only a handful of people present, you can speak to a whole room. And it's important that you make no assumptions about their responses, or lack of, while rehearsing in front of them.

Step 6, the protocol for *open rehearsals,* is almost the same, except if you have a large group, you may want to provide some type of quick and simple printed form to get each attendee's feedback. And, of course, with an open rehearsal you're going to give the greatest weight to the observations of trusted mentors and peers.

- **Choose the right people (invited rehearsal).** Focus on selecting the right people to attend when you rehearse. Why? Because you can be thrown off if the feedback isn't in the direction that you're going in. The people you choose should be good at giving supportive feedback and believe in what you're doing. In other words, find people who are sincere in their desire to help you. They shouldn't try to assert their own agenda. If you hear the phrase "Can I give you some constructive criticism?" and it's said in a snarky way, thank them, but show them the door.

- **Teach your invited guests how to take notes when you are performing.** This is crucial because it will help you after the rehearsal to digest and absorb the feedback. If you're showing them a short part of your presentation, then ask them to watch the first time through and take notes during subsequent runs. Have them write their notes in this format: "When you said 'xyz', it was unclear to me," or "I noticed that . . . ," or "I felt that . . ."

- **Ask them to note when they see an issue.** Help your guests by giving them a few things to watch for as you present your speech. For example, you could tell them, "If you see I've left a hole in my argument, when it occurs, could you find a way to object?" Or, "If I use absolutes, weak language – like *basically, sort of,* or *kind of* – or if my stories feel too detailed or don't have a resolution, please write that down." Additionally, ask them to offer you feedback on your body language, wardrobe, or hair.

- **Ask your guests to write down what's really *good* about your presentation too so you don't cut the good stuff.** Is your body language resonating with them? Is the way you use your voice – the pacing, rhythm, or timing – keeping them engaged and connected? Are you making good eye contact? What do they think of your overall presence? Which stories are most compelling?

- **Once they've seen the whole presentation, ask if they get the big idea.** Ask them point-blank to articulate the main idea or theme of your presentation. Was the content clear and did you deliver it well? Did they get the big idea? Can they clearly articulate the promise of the presentation? Do they think you delivered on the promise? It is important to get as much feedback as possible so you can decide what to incorporate into your final presentation.

Now that you have the feedback, how do you translate and incorporate it into your speech? This is tricky because you'll find that while someone will say that something is not working, he may be unable to tell you how to fix it. It's up to you to interpret what your invited guests are telling you. The way to do that is to know well what I'm teaching—then you can start interpreting. If an audience member is having trouble figuring out what you mean, it's because what you're saying isn't what you really mean. That's the vexing reality of public speaking. You have to be able to say what you mean *and make it clear so the audience knows what you mean.*

Whatever feedback you receive, take it onboard and see if you can address it. If the audience thought your story didn't work, then revisit the three-act structure or sift through the details and see what needs to be cut and what needs to be clarified. If they tell you that they had trouble hearing you, it may be time to do some voice or speech training. If they say you're not making eye contact, were you looking at the floor, or at the entire audience and not just at them? (Looking at the whole audience would, of course, be a good thing.)

Step 7: Tech and Dress Rehearsals

Dealing with Rewriting and Memorization

Most people I meet are awed by the actor's need to memorize plays, scripts, and so forth and find it somewhat intimidating. I can reassure you that by following my method, memorization will be much easier than you might think. By undertaking regular rehearsals, you will remember large chunks of your speech or pitch. The more you rehearse out loud, over and over again, the better you will know every piece of content. Still, my best advice is, when you head into tech and dress rehearsals, having your script and blocking pretty well memorized really helps. Again, that doesn't mean you have to script your presentations. Rather, it means you need to memorize structure, key points, essential details, and flow.

A few tips for making memorization easier:

- Keep everything you planned to do or say in the right order — avoid last-minute rewriting unless absolutely necessary.

- Go through your material, out loud, whenever you can, particularly during physical activity — while taking a shower, doing housework, riding an exercise bike, or taking a walk. Most neuroscientists agree that movement and cognition are powerfully connected. Amazingly, the part of the brain that processes movement is the same part of the brain that processes learning.

- Note how blocking movements ties to key passages in your text — the movement itself will help your memory.

The polished, passionate presentation you arrive at will hold up over time and can be repurposed for different uses. By the time you reach dress rehearsal, you will only want to make light edits so as to preserve the entire flow and structure. If you deliver your presentation a number of times and you receive similar comments about a particular passage, stage business, or factual error, then of course you should change it.

Tech and dress rehearsal is a simple, straightforward concept. Don't wait until the last minute to rehearse in the clothes that you'll wear during the presentation. Rather, spend as much time performing in those clothes as possible, especially the shoes. This way, you'll ensure that your clothing choices work for all elements of the performance and you'll feel comfortable during showtime.

Tech rehearsal is also often left until the last minute. However, the earlier you bring the technical elements of your presentation into rehearsal, the more comfortable you'll be on the big day. Easy management of the technical aspects is a sure sign of proper rehearsal. An audience knows you've worked hard on your presentation when they see you smoothly handling the tech pieces. If they see you masterfully moving through your slides, they're impressed. An audience loves to know that you've taken the time to prepare for a speech, meeting, or job interview, for example. They are giving you their time, and they want to know you've spent even more time in preparing for the occasion. It's a sign of respect. And it makes a difference in how they evaluate your performance.

CLOSING CONSIDERATIONS: PLAY (AND REHEARSE) WITH PEOPLE WHO HAVE YOUR BACK

In closing this chapter, I want to raise one last important question. If you're making the commitment to realize your individual potential as a performer, what about the other people on your team, in your company, or associated with your small business who will work with you during rehearsal or on the next big performance, whether that is a speech, pitch, deal, or media event? You will inevitably encounter speaking opportunities where you work with a colleague.

First, have anyone you know who may join your "cast" read this book and learn my methodology. It's important that you speak the same language of performance. If they don't know what you know, they may not be able to sync with you, or worse, they may hinder your ability to perform. But there will be times you'll need to co-present, and by showing your own commitment, you'll motivate your partner to step up his game.

And there's a more serious issue to keep in mind. You want, to the extent possible, to perform with people you like, trust, and know how to work with productively. When that is the case, you will also discover the exponential benefits of sharing in a cohesive, trusting ensemble.

You know some of the people in your life and work who have your back. You may also want to inventory who else fits this role – and who doesn't. Additionally, you'll find yourself facing business and performing situations with clients or associates you don't know well. Regardless, developing a stronger awareness about whom you'd rather have in the conference room, around your small business, and on the stage with you when the lights go up will give you the confidence to steal the show.

Playing with people who have your back means you will, wherever possible, stop working with people who wouldn't make that jump with you, who don't bring out your best, or who have conflicting interests to yours. In *Book Yourself Solid*, I used the metaphor of a red velvet rope to capture how entrepreneurs and independent professionals exercise good judgment when taking on clients. You will be more successful and productive, I argued, if you dump the clients who don't bring out your best and instead work only with clients who energize and inspire you and, most importantly, allow you to do your best work.

Book Yourself Solid has been published in multiple editions and dozens of languages and has taught the concept of the red velvet rope policy countless times. I've been told more often than I can remember that readers find the red velvet rope policy one of the most powerful and confrontational concepts in that work. It can be hard to say *no* to someone when he is saying *yes* to you. But, if it's not someone you're meant to work with, there's usually little right in the relationship and it can quickly turn to conflict and strained relations.

The initial objection some of my readers and students raise about the concept is a good one: we often can't decide whom our colleagues and/or particular clients will be. I agree that within an organization you don't always get to choose with whom you work, and as an entrepreneur you very well may need to form a strategic alliance or stage an event with someone you don't know well or someone who makes you slightly uncomfortable.

First let's recognize that being uncomfortable with a colleague may change when you get to know him; this happens all the time. But it is also a fact that if you are setting out to deliver a significant performance or product and your colleagues or co-participants don't have your back or simply lack the right chemistry with you, the outcome will suffer. That is a significant risk, and therefore, taking a calculated gamble in pushing to form the team that is right for you doesn't seem like such a stretch. If you don't, you might end up being stuck in a role you were never meant to play.

Remember, the people you rehearse with and share the spotlight with, whether in a presentation, a pitch, or a personal event, are an expression of you and they will have an impact on your performance. Think about the person you are when you are performing optimally, when you are with all the people who inspire and energize you. Now think about all the frustration, tension, and anxiety you feel when you work with colleagues or clients who are less than ideal — not so good, right?

To return to the red velvet rope analogy, think about how much you control the rope: you can make it tighter or looser depending upon the circumstances — but you should always have one. When you rehearse and perform with colleagues, partners, and teammates you like and trust, you'll truly enjoy and maybe even love the entire process. And when you love the work you're doing in the spotlight, you'll give even better performances and also bring out the best in others.

SPEED REVIEW

Effective rehearsal is the best way to keep your nerves at bay and to achieve all the potential you have for a particular performance. Adopt the seven-step protocol of:

1. Table reads: ease into your rehearsal by hearing your work out loud.

2. Content mapping: mark up your script for the spoken word by noting important words, lists, and other vocal patterns.

3. Blocking: create your plan for the intentional movements you will make during your performance.

4. Improv: experiment with your material by improvising on sequences that don't work.

5. Invited rehearsal: include a coach or peers because you will want actual training and well-informed feedback.

6. Open run-through: hold a run-through for people in your target audience (the equivalent of previews in theater).

7. Dress/tech rehearsal: make sure you are comfortable in your clothing and are easily able to handle all the technical aspects of your presentation.

And, where possible, work with people who have your back.

13

How to Produce Powerful Openings, Commanding Closings, and Amazing Audience Interaction

THIS CHAPTER INCLUDES BASIC PRINCIPLES about openings, closings, and audience interactions as well as more creative finishing touches that are useful for every presentation. I advise you to have the core of your performance nailed first, then add additional elements to motivate and delight your audience. These are strategies you can work on during rehearsal with an audience or by yourself. Over time, everyone I've coached has seen significant benefits from these approaches. They also become a lot of fun to use and instill confidence by anchoring your presentation as one that you know will start and finish strong.

In the last moments before a speech begins, there's often a certain tension as the speaker steps up to the stage or in front of a meeting. The audience, no matter how generous, will take their measure of the person in front of them. Will she bore us? Inform us? Entertain us? The speaker looks out at the space between her and the audience and feels their skepticism and hope vibrating in the air. It's the job of the speaker to break the tension as quickly as possible, win them over, and reassure them that yes, this will be worth their while.

The ending of a presentation is a different challenge: can you drive home the big idea or deliver the high-kick finish that will top off the experience with delight or surprise — and spur a wave of positive reviews, referrals, job offers, or new business?

I want my audiences to be inspired and to learn while having fun. For me, that's what interacting with the audience is all about, and I imagine the same is true for you. There are hundreds of different ways to open and close a presentation — if you're willing to take some risks and think creatively. I'll start below with powerful openings and commanding closings and then offer engaging audience interaction ideas to get you started. Grab 'em and go!

THE IMPORTANCE OF A BIO AND PREPPING YOUR PRESENTER

Don't underestimate the importance of your bio. And the bio on paper is different than the spoken bio. Of course, there are many instances where your professional bio isn't relevant to the speech you're giving: a wedding toast, a speech to other survivors of cancer, and so forth. However, in a professional setting, your bio sets the tone for your introduction, and in some ways, it determines how people respond to you. Put yourself in your audience's shoes: Are you an expert worth listening to? Are you interesting? An effective bio is short but powerful; it doesn't need to include your philosophy on a topic — that is something you communicate to the audience during your presentation.

Your bio should make you sound credible and interesting. Don't use phrases that are not verifiable. I wouldn't dare say that I was the best networker in the country. It's a pompous, general statement that isn't verifiable. However, I might include that *Forbes* listed me first of "25 Professional Networking Experts to Watch in 2015." The fact that I'm on this list is both true and verifiable. If you have accomplished something rare and impressive (climbed Mt. Kilimanjaro, have ten kids), tell the audience. And don't embellish — just tell the truth — you'll feel more relaxed delivering your presentation and won't be worried about being "found out."

One of the most important things is to prepare different versions of your bio for different audiences. What is relevant and impressive to one audience may be immaterial to another. Most people don't realize how important it is to tailor your bio to your crowd. Generally, shorter is better and more impressive. The more successful you are, the shorter your bio. We don't need to hear a bio read for Bill Clinton, Bill Gates, Oprah, or the Oracle of Omaha, Warren Buffett. There's no need to try too hard. Let your work speak for itself. But do use the bio in such a way that ensures the audience finds you credible before you walk onstage so you don't need to spend the first ten minutes proving yourself.

Writing a bio is very simple, and you can follow this formula. As you write, focus on what will make you seem credible enough to deliver on your topic.

- Describe your most significant responsibilities in your current position. When writing a first draft, include everything you do, then determine what information would be most relevant to your audience and cut the rest. Keep it short. Don't use jargon or lingo; use language that really means something to the people listening.

- Where possible, track your record and your successes. The most effective way to do this is to quantify your achievements.

- Include any other successes, unusual interests, or things that make people go *hmm*. For example, telling the audience that you love knitting and walks on the beach isn't interesting or unusual. Reserve that for a personal ad. However, if there is something exceptional you've accomplished—such as completing 100,000 puzzles—like Jeff Moore, a Book Yourself Solid Certified Coach, then share it.

Another underused opening rehearsal tactic is to prep your presenter. Of course, this is only relevant if you're giving a speech at an event where you're introduced. Before I started doing this, I can't count how many times my bio—and even my name—was mangled. A CNN anchor—who shall remain nameless—introduced me to an audience of 4,000 people as Michael *Porter* (who also happens to be an author as well as a famous professor at Harvard) instead of Michael *Port*. My advice: *Give the person introducing you exactly what you want him to read.* Tell him that if he'd like to add something at the end about why he chose you to give a speech, that's fine.

Most people don't realize it, but your presentation begins the second the presenter starts reading your bio aloud. Again, this is a point almost everyone misses, but your bio is a big part of your brand. You aren't being demanding when you ask the presenter to rehearse your bio and to follow word for word what you've written. You can even explain to her the importance of a good bio. While you are being introduced, try to be casual and relaxed, like you are part of the crowd. This is very important if you are seated in the front row, but also if you are standing off to the side of the room or of the stage.

Here's something I do that I've yet to see anyone else do (although, I have a feeling that will change since I'm including it in this book). Audiences often listen to an introduction with only one ear. They may use the time to finish up a text or a conversation with their neighbor. Since establishing credibility before a speech is so important, I often show slides while my bio is read. I show slides during the introduction so the audience focuses on the slides rather than the person reading the bio. Mind you, this is the exact opposite of what you want when you're giving your speech – that's when you want the audience focused on you. However, during your intro, you're attempting to pull focus away from the person speaking to the slides. What's on the slides? Images that represent the facts and details mentioned in the bio. Who advances the slides? You do, with the remote, from anywhere in the room.

For example, the first line of my bio often goes something like this: "Michael Port is a *New York Times* bestselling author of six books, including *Book Yourself Solid* and *Steal the Show*." At the moment that line is read, the audience sees a slide of my six book covers. Sometimes I'll use a picture of me sitting on top of all my books with a big goofy smile on my face. Then, if I include any of my acting credits in the bio, I'll show screen shots of me in those roles with actors such as Sarah Jessica Parker (*Sex & the City*) and Michael C. Hall (*Dexter*). Or, if I include my TV commentator credits from MSNBC, CNBC, or PBS, I'll show slides of me on set from various programs on those networks. This way, it makes it real. People don't always believe what they hear or it simply doesn't register. However, when they *see* something, it makes what they hear more believable and memorable.

For the adventurous, consider making your own video opening. Don't miss Ze Frank's video opening for his February 2004 TED talk – it's quite clever. (Please note: I'm recommending you watch this as an example of a video opening *only*.) You can experiment with building a video around a well-honed and rehearsed comedy bit (there's no penalty for trying). Or try a video that sets the stage and offers a little backstory on you and the topic you're about to address.

OPENING YOUR ACT

Now that you're onstage, how do you start? There are a number of openings I've heard – and I am sure you have too – such as, "I am happy to be here!" But what's the alternative? That you're really pissed that you're there? Of course you're happy to be there. Or, "We only have a little time . . ." *Oh, so, I guess that means we won't learn much,* the audience thinks.

Other clunkers I've come across: an off-topic story that doesn't land; filler material or a joke that is not related to the topic (I just flew in from Duluth — boy my arms are tired!); or even a little audience-interaction improv that isn't guaranteed to work. Sometimes the presenter will start with housekeeping notes (never use the word *housekeeping,* it signals to the audience that they don't have to listen yet). Bottom line: cut to the chase. If you're happy you're here, show them you are. If you only have a little time, don't waste it on filler.

Your entrance seems like it's a big moment because that's when the audience sees you for the first time. However, you can take it easy. If you're relaxed and can smoothly move right into your presentation, you'll be fine. You don't need to start with a story, as it's typically a clichéd way to open a speech. But that doesn't mean you shouldn't. Remember, this is art; there isn't one way to make it. You can start with a story if you know it will kill — just don't spend too long on the setup. The audience may get fidgety waiting to hear what they came for. Self-effacing humor can work well after a powerful bio, but keep in mind that there is a difference between self-effacing and self-destructive humor. I once heard a speaker attempting some self-deprecating humor start her speech by apologizing to the audience because they had to listen to her. I was so shocked, I nearly fell out of my chair.

I imagine you've heard the old adage, "Tell them what you're going to tell them; tell them; then tell them what you told them." It makes perfect sense and is completely appropriate in some situations; it can even be helpful. However, not all speeches need to open with a "here's what we're going to do today" statement. In fact, taking the audience on a journey that they don't expect can be exciting. If the speech is good, you don't need to tell them what you're going to do. When you go to see a movie, it rarely starts with the cast telling you what's going to happen for the next ninety minutes and that everyone dies in the end. And I am sure you've seen a movie trailer that ruined the movie for you. That's what can potentially happen if you don't walk a fine line.

However, for business or academic workshop situations, it really makes sense to outline what's going to happen and when, including things like breaks and lunch. And for curriculum-based presentations, there's a little more call for "here's what we're going to do." In these situations, it's not a bad approach, but there is no rule that says you must follow this structure, either.

HOW TO CLOSE A SPEECH

The closing of your speech or presentation might even be more important than the opening. You may have heard that the two things audiences remember most are their most emotional response to the speech and the closing of the speech. So, if you're presenting a curriculum-based speech, you need to provide a concise yet comprehensive short review of all the audience has learned without going into every detail.

Here are my tips for commanding a strong close: End cleanly — if anything feels like it was left unsaid, it needs to be said, but before the applause. Anything after the applause is lost as the audience has already moved on. Make sure the audience knows that you did everything you came to do. Don't say, "I'm out of time." Your presentation will feel unfinished. Additionally, even when an audience loves everything you've done and said, they often appreciate a little extra free time. Adults are just like kids in that sitting for long periods can be uncomfortable. Plus, people are busy and have things to take care of during breaks in a program.

Have you ever noticed that comedians end shows surprisingly and abruptly? That's intentional. They never want you to know what's coming next because it's a good setup for an encore. Always try to leave before the audience is ready for you to leave. Don't be the last one to leave the party. Additionally, if you're speaking on someone else's stage, possibly the most disrespectful thing you can do to the organizers, other speakers, and audience is run over your allotted time.

I gave the opening speech at a conference where two hours were allotted for six keynoters; each speaker was allotted twenty minutes. That's a tight schedule to begin with, but we're professionals; it shouldn't have been a problem. My presentation ran for nineteen minutes and forty-five seconds. The woman who followed ran for thirty-nine minutes. I kid you not. The man after her took another thirty-five minutes. It was a train wreck. The organizers were forced to cut the sixth presenter. They were none too happy and neither was the speaker. These were professionals being paid upwards of $25,000 for short speeches in front of 3,000 people. It should be obvious, but roughly 60 percent of speeches run long. I guess those speakers have more important things to say than everyone else. If it were my event, I would have pulled them off the stage.

If you have a great story to tell at the end of your performance that sums up your entire world view, then great. If you have a group activity interaction that helps you close strong—that too is great. At some point you'll want to thank or acknowledge your host, but that can be done at any point. I prefer to find a moment during the presentation to honor the people in the room and those who brought us together.

My recommendation is not to take questions at the end. It's better if the Q&A is a separate segment, if possible. I've noticed speeches where the Q&A—especially at the closing—changes the energy in the room and the presenter is no longer in control. It can work but you have to make sure that you are in control of the segment and can drive it. If you do want to include Q&A, you can do so *before* the closing and leave at least ten minutes before you end your speech so that you are completely in control of the energy and the ideas shared. In the next section, I'll share my techniques for managing the unexpected during Q&A.

TOP IDEAS FOR AMAZING AUDIENCE INTERACTIONS

You interact with your audience because interaction delivers powerful emotional and structural contrast and helps break through the outer armor of indifference people often bring to a presentation. The result is a richer, more memorable experience designed to support how your big idea can change their lives — if you go about it effectively. Don't force it. *I believe audience interaction techniques must be directly proportional to the amount of trust you've earned.* Trust takes place on two levels:

1. Your audience will trust you more as they experience the quality of your presentation and the passion you have for your topic. So, you can ask more from your audience as your performance progresses.

2. Know the baseline of trust governed by your particular situation. Are you a new manager, relatively unfamiliar to an audience of your coworkers? Are you well known within your organization? Are you well respected? Or are you somewhere in between? Are you a paid guest speaker already known to the audience, or are you relatively unfamiliar? Are you speaking to members of your local community who have a general

familiarity with you, or are you, for whatever reason, dropping in to address an unknown audience in a new place with new circumstances?

Various forms of audience interaction can require a progression of intimacy. This progression could start by asking questions and getting a show of hands, move on to asking audience members to introduce themselves to one another, progress to you going down into the audience to engage individuals, and culminate with people joining you onstage or participating in more advanced, highly interactive exercises.

You'll improve with experience in reading a room and assessing how engaged your audience is and whether you need to draw them in with more interaction. If the room or theater is dark and you can't see the audience, listen to hear if your jokes are landing — and even ask for more audible responses. ("OK, guys, I can't see all of you in the back so let me know — say *'yes!'* if you agree.") If you can see the audience, you can check them out as you go through the early parts of your performance. Remember, sometimes folks are really engaged but don't show it for any number of reasons; but if your audience looks alert and engaged and responsive, trust me, they're digging your performance.

I like to group audience interaction methods into five types: ice breakers and trust builders; reminders and reinforcers; role players; creative high-contrast exercises; Q&A tips and traps.

1. **Ice breakers and trust builders:**
    - Meet the audience before the show in the lobby or wherever appropriate. Shake hands, introduce yourself, ask names, and find out where people are from. You can take photos with them and even use the photos during your presentation, if you have time to edit them into your slides.

- Break the ice by having your audience move – stand and stretch up on their toes, do jumping jacks, move around the room if feasible. Physical exercise also improves alertness.

- Build trust by phrasing audience questions to get the desired response, which you can then tie into your next point. For example, if I'm doing my bit on what's wrong with elevator speeches, instead of asking, "How do you like giving an elevator speech?" I'll ask, "How many of you just love, love, *love* giving an elevator speech?" Some people may raise their hands if I use just one "love." However, even in a room of 5,000 people, when I use three "loves" and stretch them out, no hands go up. Have a backup plan if they don't respond as you anticipate, such as – "Good! I'm glad you love your elevator speech, and you're going to love it even more once you've heard this . . ."

2. **Reminders and reinforcers:**

- Increase engagement by asking your audience to respond to a recurring routine or question over the course of your presentation. You can have a prop you keep returning to that stands for a key idea in the presentation, say the first iPod for a speech about continuous improvement and innovation.

- Simple call and response with the audience.

3. **Role players:**

- When you have cultivated more trust in your audience, organize small groups or teams (easily done when people are seated at tables) and give each one a role relating to a major topic in your presentation. (This also works with individuals.)

- Have groups vote by moving to one corner of the room and then have each group explain their vote.

- Recruit someone from the audience to role-play a short scene with you onstage (you assign her a part), or you can move down into the house and pick someone out for a role-play or Q&A on the spot. This creates great contrast and puts you on the side of the audience. It might take a little getting used to: Like a magician looking for a volunteer, you need to pay attention to the social signals you're getting from the folks in your audience. Who is following you with their eyes or looking down or away from you? Who is leaning forward and who is not?

4. **Creative, high-contrast exercises:** When you believe your audience is ready for more involved exercises that take a larger role in your presentation, this is when you can go for it with fun ideas limited only by your imagination and common sense. Here are a few to get you started:

  - Give out prizes for the first correct answer (written or spoken) to one of your questions.

  - Toss a squishy ball with audience members to emphasize a point. (For example, I've written earlier about how improv involves being ready to pitch back a response just as you would be ready to throw back a ball after you've caught it.)

  - Put balloons on a conference table and have the audience blow them up at the beginning of your presentation. Then tell them to pop a balloon with a pen when something really resonates with them.

- Place EASY buttons on the tables: tell the audience members, "Anytime I share something that makes you think, *Wow! That was easy,* reach out and hit the button."

- Similarly, if you have access to a large whiteboard on-stage or wherever might work for that specific room, have each person write one, two, or three vital questions on the board at the beginning of the presentation. Then get the audience fully engaged by daring them to run up and mark a line through a question when you have answered it. I've done this with as many as fifty people in the room: each person wrote their top three questions about the topic on the board, and by the end of the presentation every single question was crossed off (that's as many as one hundred fifty questions answered in sixty minutes). The visual is quite powerful by the end of the session. They'll also notice that they're not alone because many of the questions or issues raised are the same. One answer might have ten people running onto the stage to cross out their individual questions.

5. **Q&A tips and traps:** A skilled speaker and performer (that means you) needs to professionally manage her Q&A sessions after a speech. As I wrote earlier, if mishandled, this portion can leave a poor final impression after all the great work you've done.

- Never say, "That's a great question!" I rarely say *never* do something, but this is an exception. If some questions are great, what are the other questions, bad ones? It's natural to get excited about a particular question and inadvertently express your appreciation. However, you can reframe your response with a little forethought. Try instead, "That's the first time anyone has asked me that," or

"That's a different way to think about it." Or, better yet, just answer the question with excitement without qualifying the worth of the question.

- If you have a questioner who is confrontational or won't give up the mic, know that, according to Freud, groups tend to normalize neurosis and your audience may fix the disrupter for you. If not, the heckler can overtake your event or normalize the group to the heckler's way of thinking. You can be gentle or fierce and need to have the discretion to know which is required and when. Say, "Thank you, I'm going to take the next question," and take the floor back. You just need to have the guts to do it. If that doesn't work, offer to answer their "longer point" after the session, if you're so inclined, and move on to the next questioner.

- For questioners who make statements or start their own speech, ask them to rephrase it as a question or just take the floor back. If you need to be fierce say, "Do you have a question or do you just want to make a statement, because this time is allotted for questions from the audience." Then paste a big generous smile across your face. Your audience loses respect for you if you let people carry on. You can cut the speechifier off with your voice, but sometimes just the gesture of a palm held in the upraised "stop" position along with a quick nod of your head as though to say "That'll do" are enough.

- For questioners who ask a question you already answered in your presentation, the gentle reproach is along the lines of, "Oh, as I answered earlier . . ." and then respond; or "I've talked about that but let me rearticulate quickly and succinctly . . ." For a questioner who persists in asking questions you've answered, you can be more pointed, "Since I covered that earlier, why don't you get the notes from somebody so I can address questions on areas not covered. Thanks so much." Other audience members will thank you; people don't want their time wasted by those who don't pay attention or come in late. However, this technique *only* works if you've addressed the issue clearly during the presentation. If you didn't, some people may need clarification. You can use the Q&A time to make sure everyone is clear.

- If a questioner starts with the phrase, "In my experience . . . ," they are not likely to ask a question, so get ready to cut them off by asking if they have a question. If not, tell them they can email you later with their suggestions or thoughts.

- In most cases, your Q&A will include lots of relevant, on-topic questions. But even when it doesn't, as I've said before, don't take down the mood in the room and leave a bad taste by humiliating or tangling with an audience member unless you have no choice in order to save your event. Make your answers super-specific, crisp, and short. Unnecessarily long answers on the speaker's part will quickly bore the audience just as they're getting eager to leave.

You've created and rehearsed your presentation. Now you're ready with the openings, closings, and audience interactions that make it even likelier that you'll steal the show. Let's move on to experience the power of improv.

How to Improvise Your Way into the Hearts and Minds of the Toughest Crowds

IMPROVISATION IS ONE OF THE MOST POWERFUL SECRETS from the profession of acting. It is a creative, nonjudgmental, open-ended approach to unscripted scenarios and live possibilities. All successful people employ improvisation to some degree, and it can be learned. Improv starts with saying *yes, and* ... It involves techniques I discussed in Part II: listening in the moment, raising the stakes, knowing who has your back, and acting *as if.* In this chapter I'll show you how it works, how to use it to perk up your performances, and how to apply its underlying capabilities to many business situations.

We tend to hear *improv* and think comedy and comedy troupes, such as Improv Everywhere, live sketch television such as *Saturday Night Live,* or brilliant talents such as Amy Poehler or Tina Fey. That may be how we know improv, but that's not all that it can do.

Improv is a mindset and trained ability useful for seizing opportunities as well as overcoming difficult situations and tough crowds with grace and class. All of us improvise; we just don't give ourselves credit for it. Improvisation always begins with your objective, which in your presentations would mean delivering it the way you wanted to and planned to deliver it to achieve the intended result. Your speech is always about the big idea you're presenting to change the world. Your objectives in meetings, interviews, pitches, and conferences will vary. Improv keeps you in the present, steers you away from *no*, and makes it okay to fail – excellent principles for workplace brainstorming sessions and even dating.

Consider the following from Tina Fey's book *Bossypants*:

> *The first rule of improvisation is AGREE. Always agree and SAY YES. When you're improvising, this means you are required to agree with whatever your partner has created. So if we're improvising and I say, "Freeze, I have a gun," and you say, "That's not a gun. It's your finger. You're pointing your finger at me," our improvised scene has ground to a halt. But if I say, "Freeze, I have a gun!" and you say, "The gun I gave you for Christmas! You bastard!" then we have started a scene because we have AGREED that my finger is in fact a Christmas gun.*

Yes, improv is something you can do on a stage with another person that is great rehearsal for situations such as interacting with your audience and running your Q&A session. (I'll also give you some great exercises at the end of this chapter.) But improv fundamentally is not about being funny. It is not about having acting talent. It's about being attentive, and having the willingness to deliver on your promises. What you see in theater and what you see in business with improv is this: the ones who commit and don't back away are the ones who produce extraordinary results.

THE IMPROV FACTOR

How does this approach really benefit you in the everyday world of your business, career, and speaking?

First, improv gives you confidence to adapt to any situation, not only presentations. You don't want to seem like a preplanned piece of cardboard in a high-stakes situation. Knowing improv means that even if you are dealing with a case of nerves, you will be cooler, looser, and more confident. Don't be that person who continues to do what she planned on doing even if the situation calls for a change in direction. When that happens, you can come across like someone having a conversation and calling the other person by the wrong name even after he's been corrected. The feeling you leave behind is, *Gee, that guy's a jerk!* Improv makes it easier for you to adjust, to be flexible and spontaneous if needed.

Twitter CEO Dick Costolo is known for his use of improv to bond with employees during various Twitter forums. "Once a week, Twitter employees meet for Tea Time," the *New York Times* reported in a profile of Costolo in 2012, "an off-the-record conversation with executives. Outsiders are forbidden. Employees say that this is where Mr. Costolo, who stands on a stage with a microphone and answers questions, shines. Sometimes the meetings are serious; other times they are rife with comedic relief."[1]

Second, a focus on improv makes your presentation more relevant to the moment as it is happening in the room. Improv creates positive, interesting moments that make for a bigger, better experience for your audience. The joke at the Transamerica event I told you about in the humor chapter ("My advice to you: send texts to your clients.") came out of using improv in the moment.

Think of the dating world. You're planning for a date on Friday night with someone whom you are very interested in and attracted to. You've made your plans, waxed your eyebrows, and picked out the perfect jazz club. You get a call Thursday afternoon from your date, whose plans have changed and offers a spur-of-the-moment dinner invitation for Thursday night, not Friday. Some of us might freeze and clear our throats and not know the next move. Of course there are many good ways to react, but the improv approach helps you respond with confidence and energy so that you move to your next goal – to go on a date with this person. So you end up accepting, showing your spontaneity, and still keeping your options open for Friday night.

Third, use improv to sharpen your skills for saving difficult moments during a performance. Speaking in public will always be about adventures in the unexpected. The venue you planned for gets changed. The laptop projector doesn't work. Your file of slides is corrupted. There's a power blackout during your presentation. Someone in the crowd passes out (this happened to President Obama during a press event in the Rose Garden). Things will and do go wrong.

I got booked for a high-profile keynote for Coldwell Banker at Lincoln Center's Avery Fisher Hall because Coldwell's marketing executive was present during a short speech I gave at an event, hosted by my friend Chris Brogan, when my visuals went down. I gave the tech guys a moment to see what they could do. But before I lost any momentum I tossed the remote up on the stage, never mentioned the glitch again, and came down and walked among the audience as I gave the same presentation (remember, you never want your slides to be cue cards that fill in important content you're not prepared to present). The Coldwell executive told me he'd never seen a speaker do that – and then do so well. (I'm sure others have, *he* just hadn't seen it before.) It was rehearsal and improv that allowed me to save the moment. I really hadn't done anything special or anything that you couldn't easily do with even a modest amount of rehearsal.

Ask my student, computer forensics expert Brian Wolfinger. Brian is a former Philadelphia cop and a huge guy — about 6'2" and 240 pounds, with a shaved head and one of those thick goatees you see relief pitchers in Major League Baseball wearing these days. His area of expertise means that Brian gives speeches to large groups of law-enforcement types. Before he took my master class, he had never worked on his speeches because he felt he was good at winging it. As he told me later, before he came to the master class, he was skeptical but he quickly realized how average his talks were. He embraced the whole rehearsal process in this book. He spent weeks polishing and refining his presentation, from big idea to closing.

Brian's speeches always involve slides, and because he addresses computer network security issues, the slides are very technical. His core speech used 120 slides. After he graduated from the master class, one of his first keynotes took place before 150 law-enforcement officers. As he got started, he looked up at the first slide and saw that the organizers had loaded the wrong presentation. So the tech person took down the slides, and it ultimately took thirty minutes to find and get the correct file loaded. However, as a result of our work together, Brian had recrafted his presentation so it was not a supplement to the slides but could be delivered independently of them. Additionally, he was so well prepared because of the seven-step rehearsal process I shared with you in Chapter 12 that he was able to roll through the presentation without rechecking his notes or losing his place. When the tech person finally got the correct slide file uploaded, Brian was able to pick up exactly where he would have been if he had used the slides all along.

His experience is a testament to the importance of rehearsal and being in the moment, especially for a professional whose life has nothing to do with professional speaking or with acting. Brian gave me a call after the keynote and said, "This is proof to me that what you guys are doing works." As you might imagine, I felt like a proud papa.

We need to be able to improvise because we're often paired with or selling to people with whom we don't always feel comfortable. We can get ourselves into trouble when we have fixed expectations in a tough sales environment. Let's say you're heading into a sales meeting where you've been working to close a deal for some time, and you've become fixated on a particular strategy that will get them to sign on the dotted line. You may have missed signals through recent developments that could have tipped you off that the landscape is changing. Suddenly you're blindsided by a change in the order, a delay, or a pass. Anyone who manages or works sales or runs his own business knows how often you think the deal is all set when the CEO steps in, your procurement manager is reassigned, or the specs change in some way.

And job interviews – you'd better expect to improvise. No matter how much you prepare, the nature of interviewing in corporations – where most professionals are not well trained in skillful interviewing and most folks outside of HR typically don't spend much time preparing for the interview – leads to surprises in format, location, process, or questions.

I'm sure you remember an interview where another executive stopped by either to do a surprise meet-and-greet with you or barge in on your interviewer with a question (again, a lot of people don't take the interview process as seriously as they should). Were you loose and ready to jump up and introduce yourself, maybe start a conversation with the guy?

I use improv to help keep me at ease if I'm meeting with a C-level executive in one company or another (this happens as part of being interviewed for speaking appearances at annual conferences or to discuss bringing our public speaking training courses into corporations). If I'm in an executive's office, I'll look around at his photos to get a sense of how ego-driven he is, which you can usually pick up if he's showing photos of himself shaking hands with celebrities or famous politicians or if he's holding a giant marlin he caught in Bimini — you get the idea. (Just for the record, I've got a few of those big fish pictures myself.) Then I'll improv a line or two that makes fun of him (not too harshly); for example, I'll point to the giant-fish brag shot and say, "That's amazing! How did you Photoshop that so well?" Showing that I see him as an equal almost always has the effect of relaxing him and taking the status issue out of the meeting.

Getting comfortable improvising will equip you with skills I assure you are all too rare. There are plenty of paid professional speakers who couldn't handle losing their slides or the lights going out or any one of many difficult situations that might happen during a performance, and your training will in this way set you apart. Even using improv for a few small changes in your performance will really stand out. Adopting improv as a daily discipline offers even more benefits. It makes you a better speaker, a better manager, and perhaps even a better person. Here's how to go deeper.

DOING MORE, GOING DEEPER WITH IMPROV

By embracing a handful of powerful ideas driven by the core techniques of saying *yes, and* . . . and others, you can improvise successfully and more frequently in more adverse and diverse situations than you have before:

Use improv to make bridges so you can go from where you are to where you want to be. The whole concept of saying *yes* is about moving action forward. That's what improv is for. It helps with all manner of public experiences, such as introductions to speeches, difficult conversations between managers and their direct reports, or pitch meetings. Being in the moment (because you've been fully prepared) frees you to fill those awkward or dead spaces between scripted portions. This taps into the core idea that to keep the action moving forward, you have to add to whatever you've been given. In an acting improv about shampoo, your counterpart might say, "I just got the greatest shampoo from my salon, and they gave me a free bottle. Do you want any?" Then you might say, "I love shampoo, I just can't use it because I'm bald. I'll use it on my chest hair, though." (Even bad jokes about being bald seem to land every time. I'm not sure why, but apparently being bald is funny.)

Improv helps you perform quickly on your feet using prepared bits for Q&A during a speaking event and in many other situations. With a little experience you'll have set answers and stories that you've found to work. When you're in the moment, you mix and match these to the question to keep bridging from one Q&A to the next, in what can seem like an effortless performance. At a wedding, you might give a toast after another member of the wedding party gives his own toast, but you build on it by thanking him for a great toast and adding a few more thoughts.

Use improv to build on *whatever* is happening *and make it better.* Rather than freezing up, use improv if something is going wrong to ask yourself, *how can I make it better?* Say there's a fire drill during a speech you're making. In that instance, you become the fire marshal. After all, you're in front of the room with a microphone. You take the lead and, if you're at a hotel, have staff find out if this is a drill or a response to an alarm, reassure the audience, and direct them to the doors. When the presentation continues, pick up where you left off without dwelling on the distraction. Improv uses our capacity to step up, lead, and make a difference, rather than hoping someone else will.

The idea of making things better also extends to your content. When you improvise you should make others look good. You don't want your improv to be sarcastic or at anyone else's expense. The kind of improv I'm talking about isn't standup comedy. You have to get other people to *want* to come with you. Think of how well this works in terms of dating. With the *yes, and . . .* approach, your date's embarrassing story is a cue for you to tell an embarrassing story about yourself; your date's miscue or misstatement isn't awkward but a *yes, and . . .* moment for you to keep the conversation going and to connect over a similar experience.

Use improv to stay mindful and tuned in. The more you are inclined to say *yes, and . . .*, to act *as if,* and stay in the moment on a daily basis, the more you will notice, the better you will pay attention, and the more mindful you will be of what others in your life are saying and doing. Yes, the improv principles lead you to a kind of mindfulness where you have more presence and live more in the present. Employing these principles actually works when you do it consistently. Try it in your next boring meeting and see what happens.

Use improv to ask, are you in or are you out? I like that learning to say *yes, and . . .* is about finishing what you started. In improv, actors are taught not to prejudge: you jump in, jump in deep, and find out what works. You become much more engaged in making things happen than in questioning *why* things happen to you. The commitment to keep at it that improv requires can make for a clarifying and refreshing change from the half-assed nature of many business transactions. My view is that too many times in business and other realms people say things they don't mean, make promises they don't intend to honor, or just don't care enough to finish strong. And to be fair, people often hold back on a commitment if they sense they will be unfairly judged or evaluated. Introducing improv principles and techniques is an excellent antidote to this kind of malaise in a workplace or team. It keeps folks in the moment and creates a positive space where colleagues know their ideas won't be shot down. You can start a new meeting, say, with an improvisation exercise about revamping the company's website or social media strategy. You begin planning for the department's presentation at the annual sales conference with an improv exercise aimed at putting untried ideas on a whiteboard. As the improv goes around the table, no one is excluded.

Of course there's a place to challenge, ask questions, and push back against the status quo, but too often this is the easy way out of not following through on a commitment. Through improv you can rediscover what children learn from playing games in the third or fourth grade. Either you are in, or you are out.

This aspect is incredibly important to what you do in your speeches. If your audience can sense that you're not 100 percent committed, they will turn you off. I've seen it happen many times. If a time comes when you are scheduled to speak and you are distracted by a business problem or a personal worry or a pressing deadline, use the principles as I have done at times — act *as if* this is the biggest speech of your life. True, you may have to imagine that. But raise the stakes, and remember that you have people out there in your network and family who will have your back. That's improv too.

DOING THIS STUFF BEATS READING THIS STUFF

I can write all day about improv, but to really get it you need to work at it. Improv is popular in business consulting circles because corporations (particularly larger ones) and many organizations struggle with encouraging or even tolerating team building, spontaneity, creative problem-solving, and grassroots innovation unless the process fits squarely inside organizational charts and expectations. In fact, recently I had a discussion with leaders of the innovation team at one of the world's largest and most innovative car companies about bringing improv workshops into their department. Why? They'd tried all the typical corporate team-building experiences, but the innovation team still wasn't feeling particularly innovative. They needed to rediscover their spontaneous, creative thinking and they felt improv could help. They were right. There's only so much you'll get from improv by thinking about it. A day's worth of exercises at your corporate retreat can be a good start, as can this book. But it won't matter unless you can make this approach part of how you live and do business. So toward that end, I'll close this chapter with exercises and ideas that consistently work in my classes and in my experience.

IMPROV STARTERS AND EXERCISES

- One exercise is the story-story game. It's done with your group, however large or small, arranged in a circle. The group is given a theme: a children's bedtime story, a spaghetti Western, a reality TV show, or any other scenario that gives the players a sense of setting, time, and place, along with an opening line like, "The cat jumped over the moon." One person begins building upon the opening line, and at a critical transition moment, the facilitator says "Next," and the next person picks up the thread and continues building the story. The game continues quickly with no breaks until the facilitator calls it to a close. This simple format can also be used to teach storytelling by having the first person create act one, the present circumstances; then the second person creates act two, the conflict; and the third person delivers the resolution. You can go around the circle and improve the stories in this way. Enjoy this compelling, popular method to use improv. You can also play this game by having each person add only one word. That's my favorite way to play. It's something that Amy and I do while on long plane trips. I can't imagine how many people we've woken up with our uncontrollable laughter.

- I use what I call the gibberish game to great success. Break a group of participants into pairs or have them take turns. One participant plays an alien from another planet who doesn't know any earthly language and verbally is limited to gibberish — vocalizations of any kind as long as they aren't words — and all the body language she can possibly use. The paired participant plays the translator. The alien is given a message to get across, such as "I need to bring three million Big Macs and fries to my planet. Our spaceships run on grease." She quickly figures out that to communicate, she's going to have to improvise all manner of intense, wild, and super-animated body language to have any chance of being understood by the translator. Typically, when people playing the alien go bigger and really bounce off the walls with their energy, they have more success. For the translator, he'll be guessing at the alien's content, which makes for some hysterical "translations" that the assembled group will enjoy. Taking away the requirement to use English allows folks to break out.

- The tell-me-a-secret game requires at least two people but can include as many people as you want. In the game, each person tells a secret that is either true about himself or true about a friend as if it were his own secret, or he fabricates a secret. It's a fascinating game in that it gives people the opportunity to open up and express themselves in meaningful ways.

- In the whiteboard challenge, you start a staff meeting by writing a goal on the whiteboard that is meaningful to your team. It could be to increase sales 10 percent by the fourth quarter, double web traffic to the CEO's blog, develop a new menu item within a set amount of time, open two new yoga studios, finance a café next to your bookstore, whatever would be a game-changing result for your team or business. You start at one end of the table and ask for the first person's suggestion to move toward that goal. Then, the next person uses *yes, and* ... to connect to or expand the idea without refuting it or going in an entirely different direction. Keep going around the table a couple times until you have a few actionable initiatives to explore.

- The Internet and your local library offer books and resources packed with dozens of group improv games for the workplace and classroom. Many are simple and appropriate for nonactors. Using short vocalization or improv games to warm up an important meeting or conference changes the tone and frees up a lot of energy.

- Many of the tips in the previous chapter for audience interaction activities can be used in workplace meetings as well.

In 2011, the Emmy Award–winning actress Amy Poehler gave a speech at Harvard University's Class Day that went viral. The speech was about how the particulars and secrets of live comedy and improv have sustained her through a long and acclaimed career in television and film. But she was speaking to everybody there, not just actors, like what I'm doing with this book.

In deconstructing the elements of good comedy, Poehler made some smart observations about the mindset of improv: "I moved to Chicago in the early 1990s and I studied improvisation there," Poehler said. "I learned some rules that I try to apply still today. Listen, say yes, live in the moment, make sure you play with people who have your back, make big choices early and often. Don't start a scene where two people are talking about jumping out of a plane. Start the scene having already jumped. If you are scared, look into your partner's eyes. You will feel better."

SPEED REVIEW:

- Improv is a mindset based in saying *yes, and* . . . , a trained ability that goes far beyond comedy.

- Improv gives you confidence to adapt to any situation.

- Improv makes your presentation more relevant to the moment.

- Every speaker faces difficult situations and surprises at some point — improv is great training for saving those moments during a performance.

- We need to be able to improvise because we're often paired with or selling to people we don't feel comfortable with.

- Improv as a discipline improves mindfulness and fosters the ability to build on whatever is happening to find ways to make it better.

How to Get a Standing Ovation Every Time — Really

YOU KNOW HOW TO TAKE ON AN AUTHENTIC ROLE to fit the moment. You know how to silence your critics. You know your structure. You know the promise you're going to make to the audience. You know the big idea they will want to act on when they leave the room. Your opening is ready. Whether it is a story, joke, observation, or fact, it comes from a place of certainty and strength within you that you'll find easy to speak about. You know your blocking. You've polished your closing, and you appreciate the power of improvisation.

It's time to master the big move to the performance itself, with tips and strategies for connecting at a psychological, practical, and emotional level with your audience through my five keys to a show-stealing performance. They are the pre-show ritual, developing stage awareness, owning the room, creating intimate moments, and managing the post-show cycle. These are your playbook for turning your rehearsed presentation into an actual live event that fulfills its potential. Oh, and somewhere along the way, I'll tell you how to get a standing ovation every single time. *Every time.* Yes, that's what I wrote.

THE FIVE KEYS TO A
SHOW-STEALING PERFORMANCE

1. The Pre-Show Ritual

A big part of preparing for your live speech, job interview, or sales pitch is taking care of all the not-so-obvious details that can make or break your big moment. They include understanding the space in which you'll perform, prepping the event's organizer, and managing the audience if things don't go your way. My philosophy? Always be prepared because if anything happens (and things do happen), you'll be able to get back on track.

If you don't have a pre-show process, I bet you would like to have one. The days before a major performance bring a lot of anticipation and nerves and your mind may be leaping around from one idea to another. My system for dealing with a bad case of nerves is based on traditions and acting best practices along with my own experience and that of many of my colleagues and clients: dry and tech run-through, vocal and physical warmup, and smart dos and don'ts when it comes to what to eat and drink before you go on.

A dry run is simply a run-through of your speech at 50 percent so you don't tire yourself out before the big moment. Make sure to run through all the blocking and use of props. A tech run-through is just as it sounds, an opportunity for you to run through the technical elements of your presentation. Plan for a dry run and tech run ideally on the day of the performance, and pay special attention to the people who run visuals, sound, and lights. Identify whom your go-to person will be if there's a problem during the presentation.

If you're prepping for a deal or investor pitch in offices you won't be able to see before the meeting, see if you can find a comparable space, maybe in the hotel where you're staying, and do your run-through and tech check. Ensure that your tech is reliable, with backup laptops loaded with your slides or at least thumb drives with backup files in case of glitches.

I cannot stress enough the importance of going through a dry run. Why? Because by running through your performance from top to bottom, you'll not only feel more comfortable, both with the material and the setting, but you can iron out any remaining kinks during that process. Remember, this is a run-through; you're conserving your energy for the main event. Think of it as pre-programming your muscle memory.

Effectively Working with Event Organizers

In Chapter 13 we discussed the importance of prepping the organizer with your bio before your big moment, but there is a whole host of things you should share with her before you take center stage: all your materials, equipment needs, audio-visual specs, aspect ratio of screen, remote, microphone, lighting, collateral, whose computer you'll use, backups, finding your light, tech rehearsal (when and how?), support staff (video and sound engineers). Make sure the people around you are prepped and ready to help. Once you're onstage delivering your speech, all the supporting things you'll need should do what they're supposed to do seamlessly.

In working with the organizer, you want to be easy to work with, but you don't want to be a pushover either. Ask for what you need — and be as specific as possible. If she asks you why you need something, reassure her that it's because it will make the show great. I do it (and I mean it). I say, "This is why my show is going to be awesome."

Details matter at this stage, even with something as simple as where to place the microphone. First, as noted earlier, understand that there are different types of mics — wireless hand-held, wired hand-held, lavaliere, and countryman (lightweight, over-the-ear mic with a slender mouthpiece that also connects to a mic pack). Figure out what's available and which type you'd like to use. Also figure out the placement of the mic pack and the wire if you're using a lav or a countryman. When using a lav, in most cases, you'll run the mic wire under your shirt and clip the mic 6 inches below the center of your neck or on your collar if need be. However, when using a countryman, you may run the wire up under the back of your shirt. *Tip:* Once you've got your mic on, make sure it's turned off before you go into the bathroom. I could tell you some stories . . .

And once more for emphasis: The people behind the scenes are crucial to your presentation, so tell them how great they are to work with. Appreciate them. Let them know that you can't do your job without them.

You know that expression — timing is everything? With speeches, you may not have the luxury of choosing the ideal time to deliver yours, but once you know where you are in the lineup, you can plan accordingly. Find out what time of day you're speaking and where you are in the order of the presenters. If you are presenting first, you can work in a brief shout-out to the other speakers and the program that will follow you. If you are presenting last, you don't have to thank the organizers to the extent everyone else did. If you do, keep it short. When you're up last, you want to a greater degree than the others to cut all the filler and finish ahead of time.

You don't need to make crazy changes because of the people before you, but understand the context that surrounds the other speeches presented so you can address it if necessary. Don't be disappointed if you are the last to present. It fact, at many conferences, the most desirable slots are first and last.

And finally: Keep in mind who will have your back. If you're invited to speak on a conference panel, schedule an early call with the other invited speakers and see what you can learn about their approaches and their plans. You often can tell fairly easily from the nature of the conversation with whom you will click, who may attempt to upstage you, or who is lacking the motivation to do a great job. I believe in people. I really do. It's my concept of spiritual connection. Nonetheless, reality demonstrates that not everyone has your best interests at heart. It happens. Establishing early communications gives you time to prepare, even if you are stuck with a particularly difficult lineup. Word to the wise: it's one thing to recognize that this will probably happen from time to time; it's another thing to base your worldview on the idea that everybody is out to get you. If that's your perspective, it's going to be hard to find people who are willing to have your back. It's hard to earn trust without extending it yourself.

Similarly, make sure you organize early rehearsals for speaking appearances or press events where you're unclear about how you will work with the rest of your cast members. As you experience that process you'll be able to adjust. If you begin to notice that someone could be a problem, see if you can limit their role, or if you truly sense a disaster in the making, explore options for renegotiating or reorganizing the commitment or cast members.

If you're going to be a performer, you want people around you, people who have your back, because you'll have to go out on a limb again and again. That's what I've been talking about consistently in this book. You're going to take big chances. Do you know whose eyes you can look into when you make the jump? Do you know who will catch you if you have a bumpy landing?

Warmup Routine

Many actors, sports figures, and other well-known people follow a set routine in the hours just before they deliver a performance. Professional baseball players shag flies and take batting practice. NFL teams run through their plays without pads and wearing only helmets. Ballet dancers limber up and do their barre exercises. The pre-show warmup serves a couple of purposes: most performers

(even the big stars) have some nerves, and a familiar routine is com-
forting and for many a good luck charm; it's also important to get
your voice and body ready.

I have heard that Bruce Springsteen doesn't do vocal warmups
before his concerts (his wife, Patti Scialfa, does), but he usually
will play an acoustic song for early arrivals as a warmup. When the
Broadway and film actress Patricia Clarkson is reporting for an eve-
ning performance, she'll have a light meal, eating by four o'clock,
and get to the theater early. (Her post-show ritual? Bourbon and
French fries.) Before a stage performance, actress Martha Plimp-
ton does about twenty minutes of meditative stretching to get her
breathing in order and manage pre-show anxiety and fear.[1] NFL su-
perstar receiver Calvin "Megatron" Johnson warms up pregame
with yoga for "stretching, to relieve physical pain, and as a way to
relax before shredding a secondary."[2]

I'll do a short physical limbering up for fifteen minutes (stretching) and another five minutes of vocal work. After delivering
speeches for so many years, I find I don't need as much warming
up as I used to. Muscle memory again. I will, if at all possible, make
time for meeting attendees outside or inside the room before the
event (see Chapter 13 on audience interaction). Having this social
contact works for me; it helps me loosen up, relax, and stay conversational. After you've finished your pre-show ritual, I recommend
turning to whatever keeps you loose and conversational, whether
that is listening to music, doing a crossword puzzle, chatting with
colleagues, or grooving with a Hula-Hoop.

Finally, here are some basic pre-show dos and don'ts that may
seem obvious to some but are not well known:

- Do have a light meal at least two hours before your performance.

- Do choose easily digestible foods that settle your stomach.

- Don't eat spicy or heavy foods that will distend your stomach or cause discomfort.

- Do hydrate with water or herbal teas.

- Don't have caffeinated beverages at least one hour before your performance: I've known lots of folks who thought quaffing a venti from Starbucks or a can of Redbull would provide a timely jolt of energy, only to make themselves over-charged and jittery for the actual performance. Trust me, your adrenaline will already have you on full alert. Further-more, caffeine tightens the vocal chords and can constrain vocal quality.

- Avoid all dairy foods except in tiny quantities (like a little milk in your tea) the day of your performance; dairy gener-ates mucous in most people and will affect vocal quality.

- Remember what we said about wardrobe—you should have decided on your clothes well ahead of the performance, and you should have rehearsed wearing them. But if you've cho-sen a new wardrobe, set out your clothes before you take your shower for the day so there's no anxiety about it.

The next key is understanding and adjusting for the space you'll be using—call it stage awareness.

2. Developing Stage Awareness

Many people underestimate the impact of the performance space on the presenter. If you've seen a play, you know that the space around the actor and how she uses and fills it is important to her performance. By knowing your space you make it easier to adjust your movements and communicate more effectively with your audience. For example, if your presentation space is much larger than the stage you rehearsed on and has more rows of seats, you need to adjust your blocking so your movements expand to cover the farther points of stage left and stage right.

Common performance spaces include conference rooms at hotels, theater-style auditoriums, standard classrooms, restaurants or bars, living rooms, exercise or yoga studios, high school auditoriums, and outdoor courtyards, among many others. Each space will have its nuances, so once you know where you're performing, get to know the layout. Some conference rooms in hotels have risers that are 12 to 18 inches off the floor. Check that the risers are stable during your tech rehearsal. The last thing you need is unsteady feet as you walk up to the stage with all eyes on you. If you learn that your performance space has a theater layout, keep in mind that the stage can be situated lower than the audience and you will need to be vigilant to play to the back of the house. If you'll be in a video conference, the action will be projected onto a screen. If you move around a lot in your blocking, prep the video team on what they can expect.

The other part of understanding your performance space is being aware of audience placement. Here's the first rule of seating arrangements: If there are more seats than people, strike the empty seats from the rear. You can verify before the presentation with conference organizers to confirm projected attendance. If the room is below capacity, use your perfectly adequate math skills and tape off a conservative number of rear rows as if they are reserved; then, as people enter, guide them to the front, where you want them to sit. As the front rows are filled, if you need more capacity, take tape off the back rows as needed. If it is unknown how many will attend, make an educated, conservative guess and tape off the appropriate number of rows. If more people need seats, same thing, just remove the tape. There are other seating styles you should be aware of: class-room, theater, round table, and horseshoe styles. Where needed, observe the principle of seating people closer to where you're performing.

As part of your dry run, think through the basics of your stage movement in the actual space you'll inhabit:

- Where will you mentally draw the line of standing too close to your audience or inadvertently posing for the dreaded crotch shot?

- What is your span of eye contact?

- What movements can be larger, which smaller? As always, use gestures that feel natural.

As the person on stage, it's your job to manage your performance — and by extension, the audience. A big part of doing that will come from the energy of being onstage. Performers respond when they're in front of an audience, but the energy in a room can change with a blink of an eye, so you have to be ready for anything that happens. Be prepared. Be primed for it so you can control it. That's what the third key is about: how to own the room.

3. Owning the Room

Thinking that something might go wrong with your performance can create anxiety and may even make you more anxious when you are onstage. Don't panic. Just try to be helpful to the audience and connect with people — even if it's just one person you pick out of the crowd or whom you can visualize as a friend. These are times to draw on a role you've played before that is authentic to you — the coach, the tough teacher, the savvy sales leader — to sharpen your psychological edge. In the long run, the only way to get over your nerves is to get as much experience as possible presenting in front of crowds. The better you think you are, the more comfortable you'll get, so don't spend too much time listening to the critics and know good things are coming to you.

So, how can you begin to get comfortable? Three words: *Own the room.* Own it physically, energetically, emotionally, and psychologically. The skills and mindset required to consistently own the room through confidence mature over time. It's a mastery you achieve in levels.

Reassure the Audience

First, you start owning the room when the audience knows that they are protected and in safe hands. You've got this covered because you've rehearsed and mastered your presentation or pitch, you're committed to handling the unexpected, you're starting off with your most comfortable and confident bits, and you're at ease with your costume and props. Even if you're nervous, your audience will relax in the presence of this kind of preparation.

These techniques also help build your confidence and theirs in you. Always try to set the ground rules (such as no texting) in the beginning. Be forthright and not wishy-washy. You don't want to make it appear that you are fighting for the audience's attention. If you ask your audience to do something, wait until everyone has done it. If you skip over or forget a chunk of your presentation, sometimes it's more important to maintain the flow, logic, and command of your speech than to retrieve the missing chunk. Don't go back for it unless it will work sequentially with your content or you could lose your place in the speech. If you absolutely need what you skipped, introduce it as an "add on," share it, and come right back to where you were. No need to tell the audience it was something you forgot.

And, if you don't go back to it, there is certainly no benefit in telling the audience what they're not getting.

Keep in mind that you need to attend to the whole room. You will no doubt experience speaking in certain settings where the combination of bright stage lights and dim house lights means you won't see many faces out there in the seats. Stay conscious of speaking to *the entire house*. It can help to visualize speaking to a friend or loved one sitting up there in one of the more remote seats. Shine your joy and confidence as a performer directly out to those upper rows of the performance space.

Command with Physical Presence

The next level of owning the room is commanding the audience with your physical presence. If an audience member is talking too loud, making a fuss getting into his seat, or otherwise breaking the mood in the room, don't explain, ask forgiveness, or apologize. Use silence to quiet someone. Wait until they've stopped making noise. Do not compete with them. You can use your hand to indicate that they need to stop. Good speakers require that you listen to them and will not speak if there's noise in the room. If you are in a pitch meeting or major sales call and your counterparts are taking calls, rustling papers, or darting in and out of the office, pausing and remaining silent until they shut up (frankly speaking) and *only then resuming* gives you command of the situation. You may be surprised by my use of strong language: *require, demand, own.* That's how I want you to think. That doesn't mean that you are obnoxious, arrogant, or disrespectful in any way whatsoever. But I do want you to feel like you're in charge during your speech. It's a powerful feeling and it has a huge impact on your performance.

Take note: You can expect house noise at the opening of your presentation. Be prepared for it. This is good practice, as well, because you'll be ready to deal with it. If you open your remarks and the house is still loud, you stop, say nothing, pause, and, if needed, raise your hand. Then simply say, "Thank you."

Once you have that situation under control, be happy to be there, no matter how nervous you are. Take whatever anxiety you may be feeling and channel that into your voice and body language with a few degrees of extra exuberance. The key is to *show* the audience how happy you are. Don't *tell* them that you are happy to be there. You can show and even tell them that you're nervous as long as you focus on what you're there to do. Take a breath. Get it under control. The only way they will let you be a leader is if you can control yourself. If you can control yourself, they will allow you to control the room. If you're talking to anyone—a tech person, answering during a Q&A, or even dealing with a heckler—and you look flustered, you've lost the room. If the audience sees that you have a high level of emotional and social intelligence, they immediately find you more powerful and are more likely to quickly and willingly offer you their respect.

The Vocal Instrument

There's one more aspect of your physical presence I'd like to address: your *voice*. When trained, your voice is a remarkably persuasive and captivating instrument—it can become a significant ally. As I'm sure you know by now, your tone of voice can powerfully influence how others feel. The human voice requires training and practice for full expression, as with any instrument, and embarking on that effort cannot easily begin in the pages of a book where I can't hear you (like I said earlier, it would be creepy if I could!) and vice versa. But I want to raise your awareness. You want to attain a free and open voice. This voice is well supported by your breath; it is natural, without any artificial affectation, and not constricted by anxiety. The free and open voice is driven by your need to communicate something and connect with the audience.

To get familiar with what we call *voicework*, you must learn more about accessing and using all of the "resonators" that add register, range, and power to your voice—your chest, mask (face), and head voices. Put your hands on your body to feel the vibration when you make these sounds:

- *Huh* (you should feel this sound in your chest)

- *Meeeee* (you should feel this nasal sound in your mask)

- *Kiiiii* (you should feel this sound move up from your mask to your head)

- Sigh out, vocalizing *heeeeeeeeeey* using different pitches and feel the voice move from chest to head

- Using sound, blow out through your lips, trying different pitches each time.

- Practice saying aloud the sounds of *a-e-i-o-u* and again pay attention to the resonators and how they vibrate (use the pure sounds, not the names of the letters).

Listen and notice how you and the people around you use voice and how that makes you and others feel. You might find that you feel one or two of the resonators more than the others. That's natural. You might also discover that you would be well served by doing voice training with a coach. If you feel constricted in your throat, overly nasal, or you tend to lose your voice, some regular training in breathing and voice techniques can really make a big difference. Even simply paying more attention to this dynamic will teach you a lot. The voice I use for my son when I say, "Jake, you're about to cross the line," has immediate impact: Dad's getting pissed and is really trying to control himself. Imagine your boss saying these different phrases and what his tone of voice would instantly tell you: "Joe,

could you stop by my office for a moment when you have a chance?"
or "Joe, see me in my office," or "Joe, come over to my office, you
have *gotta* see this." If you'd like, go to www.HeroicPublicSpeaking
.com, where you'll find a video of Amy and me demonstrating voicework techniques. And if you need additional help, just let us know.

Provoking Your Audience

A more sophisticated level of owning the room lies in the idea of
provoking your audience, getting them to take risks, and taking risks
yourself while still making them feel safe. Take the biggest risks you
can, but be careful because you don't want the audience to be worried about you while you are presenting. If you do stress them out,
you'll lose them, and they will no longer hear you.

Don't worry — I'm not suggesting you improvise a soliloquy in
iambic pentameter or do an impromptu handstand. Provoking a
deeper buy-in from the audience involves interactions that fall
along a spectrum of low-key to bold and includes controlled moments of improvised confidence. Many of the audience interaction
techniques I described in Chapter 13 apply here, such as

- Tell a well-crafted, well-rehearsed joke. When it draws a
  strong laugh, you pause and acknowledge that it took you
  some time to build up the courage to tell a joke onstage and
  you're glad you nailed it.

- Pause and say, "Say *yes* if you agree," and listen for the *yes*-
  ses. Call on an audience member who agrees to explain why
  she does.

- Reveal a part of your backstory that shows vulnerability, such
  as an addiction or childhood trauma, and briefly explain how
  you overcame it. Pass it on to the audience to consider how
  their own vulnerabilities play into their life stories and careers.

- Use a short video that sets up a point that is funny, offbeat, or revealing, such as a clip from a movie (like the example from the film *Swingers* that I use below); twenty or thirty seconds from a home movie of you as a child (for instance, if you want to make a point about tapping the power of creativity in success and how we're all creative as children, you could show a clip of you doing imaginative dress-up play when you were six years old); or any number of options that are personal, funny, or powerful — as long as the clips are short, not offensive, and tested beforehand.

Finally, when you have finished your presentation, accept and enjoy the applause. Then, when it's time to leave, turn and go. Don't linger or look back.

Let's now turn to the fourth key: creating intimate moments.

4. Creating Intimate Moments

There's no explicit rule for how you produce emotional moments with your audience. You already know your material through the creative process and rehearsal, right down to the beats and blocking of your movement. You know where you've geared up to hit your audience emotionally. You know where you've struck a chord with people in other presentations and rehearsals. You want to develop an awareness of your audience's mood and receptivity so they are open to the various textures and messages of your presentation.

For the emotional touchpoints in your remarks, timing is just as important as it is with jokes. Let the moment land. Most speaking teachers tell you to slow down. Sometimes that makes sense, but if we're worried about speed, we're focused on the wrong thing. Instead of slowing down, focus on *pausing* for high points. Speakers who speak too slowly have a sedative effect. I speak quickly. And I pause at the right places. That creates rhythm. I slow down when it serves the speech to slow down. Remember how contrast creates compelling theatrical experiences? Audiences can easily absorb the most emotional points, even if you're speaking quickly, if you give them time to consume what you've shared. Also, remember that one note, even the most beautiful note, is hard to listen to over time, or at least it gets a bit boring. Vocal variance helps influence how the audience feels.

Many Academy Award and Golden Globe acceptance speeches offer helpful micro-examples of how to create intimate moments. Of course, there have also been some real clunkers. So, you see, just because one can act, it doesn't guarantee one can give a killer speech. Without a carefully crafted and well-rehearsed speech, even an Academy Award–winning actor won't be ready for his big moment if he plans on winging it. However, some actors, in these situations, succeed at sharing a powerful, authentic emotion to connect with the audience. When Meryl Streep won for Best Actress in *Iron Lady,* she created an intimate moment to diffuse the potential disappointment the audience might feel in her winning yet again and to thank particularly her husband and her colleagues. "When they called my name, I had this feeling I could hear half of America saying, 'Oh no. C'mon. Why her? *Again?*' But whatever . . . First I'm going to thank Don, because when you thank your husband at the end, they play him out with the music . . . The thing that counts to me is the friendships and the love and the sheer joy we have shared making movies together, my friends." In Michael Keaton's praised speech at the 2015 Golden Globes, he was open about his joy and gratitude, remembering his roots as the seventh child of hard-working parents in western Pennsylvania who saw a lot of tough times. He was tearful in thanking his "best friend," his son, Sean, and in speaking about how much the role in *Birdman* had meant to him. He contained the moment wonderfully, transitioning to thank the cast and director.

In my *Think Big Revolution* keynote, I show a video clip of a photographer who takes pictures of strangers on the street in intimate poses: holding hands, one person's head leaning on another's shoulder, or even hugging. It's quite moving. It demonstrates how quickly intimacy between people can be created if they're willing to let it happen. So, of course, I have my audience do the same. I break them up into groups of four, instruct them to take out their smartphones and mirror the poses they saw in the video. During the exercise, I have pictures of the various poses running on the screen with music playing in the background. Of course, I'm crystal clear in my instructions regarding how it's going to start and end, how long they'll be doing it, and exactly what they're supposed to do. I've done this with thousands of people in massive convention centers and it has always worked brilliantly. People just love it.

Get a feel for managing and understanding your energy level and the audience's. When you are onstage or facing a room full of people, feel where they are with you and the content. Do they settle down right away? If you see smiles and folks leaning forward, exhibiting the behaviors of active listening, they're with you — absolutely. If you find that the audience is dragging, get them up on their feet right away with an interaction such as asking for a standing ovation for the event sponsor or an element in your presentation.

Let's say you're giving a speech about mentoring and you have a passage along these lines that a friend of mine wrote: "As a teen, I went through a very troubled time when I was at risk, and the appearance of a wonderful mentor — a theater teacher — helped change my life. At other times in my career, I've benefited from extraordinary mentoring. More than ever, I believe firmly that investing in supports for young people, such as mentors combined with training and a path to higher education, is one of the urgent imperatives for our time." If you have sensed that your audience is sluggish at this point, you could then offer: "I'm sure many of you in this audience have had a mentor who changed your life. With that person in your mind, let's give all the mentors in our lives a standing ovation." You always want something of this kind in your back pocket that will get them up and moving.

Whatever happens, do not let it appear that you are trying too hard to get the audience on your side or to do something they don't want to do. To keep the audience's attention, you must appear calm and in control. Finally, let's review how to preserve your emotional connection to the audience and maintain your resilience and purpose if aspects of your presentation go wrong.

Emotional Resilience When Moments Go Wrong

There are three types of performers: those who have bombed, those who haven't yet but will, and those who have but lie about it. Sooner or later it may happen to you. You'll have the sinking feeling that your jokes aren't landing, your points are flying over the heads of your audience, or you've caught your audience on a day when they just found out their company is being audited by the IRS. No matter how it seems in your head at the moment, you have worked very hard to give your speech that day. People in the room are taking in your message and still can be reached. It's almost always not going as badly as it might seem to you in the moment.

My advice for those moments is simple: *let go, move ahead with your material, and don't look back.* Don't repeat the mistake made by the main character in the late 1990s film *Swingers.* Director and actor Jon Favreau plays Mike Peters, a nice guy coming off a six-year relationship who meets a woman he really likes. He calls and leaves her a message on her answering machine about getting together. He doesn't like his nervous manner, so he calls again but only makes it worse when he rambles and is cut off by the machine. The comedy builds as he calls again and again, trying to explain himself while his messages become more painfully awkward and desperate with every try. The woman eventually picks up the phone (those were the days when you actually heard the message being left on the machine) and says, "Don't ever call me again."

Even if you bungled or bombed one segment of your presentation, don't call back to leave another message. The truth is, most people remember the most emotional moment and the last part of a speech; the flub in the middle that's looming like a mountain in your mind won't typically be remembered by most of your audience. Of course, most of us are sensitive and a bit insecure about our performances regardless.

In the vast majority of circumstances where an audience is attending your presentation for business, professional, or community reasons, the speaker can't read how the audience thinks she's doing. Sometimes you'll nail an interview but walk out of the office thinking you bombed. You might even bumble through a sales pitch or negotiation but find that you closed the deal. Actors will tell you that they often get standing ovations for what they believed were their worst performances, and so it is with other types of performances too. Even if you have your doubts about how well you're doing, do your best not to show that. You can close out the performance experience with positive, proactive steps and address what worked and what needs improvement analytically during the post-show cycle, the fifth key.

5. Managing the Post-Show Cycle

Naturally, the end of your performance, of any kind, is also the beginning of improving your next one. If the performance is a speech, don't rush to leave how you're feeling — whether you're up, discouraged, or somewhere in between. If the performance is a high-stakes deal pitch or job interview where you're not embedded in a larger event, decompress over lunch, coffee, or a drink with a colleague or supporter. Remember all the good work you've invested and know that your career and the world are a better place for your commitment and the talent you've shared.

Managing the post-show cycle has three phases: the graceful exit, the thoughtful follow-up, and the balanced analysis. Let's look at these in order. First, the graceful exit:

- Leave a great final impression. After your strong finish, if you have the opportunity, walk among and talk to as many audience members as possible. Answer questions and let people share their ideas about your subject matter. You had your time onstage, now give others the floor, especially if they disagree with you. Just airing their thoughts will make them feel good about their ideas and better about your speech, even if they didn't agree with everything you said. Don't get into any debates, just listen.

- Make sure to thank everyone involved, especially the tech team. Don't just throw your mic on the podium or leave it somewhere on the platform.

- If you used a laptop, remember to take it with you. I've left a few behind in my day.

- Giving a speech can be emotionally draining. Eat something nourishing after your performance and get some rest, but make sure you don't just retire to your hotel room right away, especially if you aren't feeling great about the performance. Isolation can make you feel worse. As I've already said, in most cases it's better for you to touch base with a colleague, friend, or mentor. Holing up in your room often starts the negative analytical process of picking apart your performance.

The second aspect is the thoughtful follow-up. After the event, send handwritten cards and gifts to the organizers and anyone else who helped make your speech, interview, or sales meeting successful. Recently, I worked with a company that had a gift bag waiting for me in my hotel room upon my arrival. With excitement, I opened the bag to find a bottle of red wine, some fancy coffee, and a few bags of cookies. Unfortunately, I don't drink wine or coffee and I don't eat sweets (I know, I'm a bit of a bore). It was the stock corporate gift. It wasn't personalized so it didn't have the intended effect. I really hope I don't sound ungrateful using this as an example because I'm not. I'm tremendously grateful for any gift I'm given. I share this story with you so that when you send gifts, it is clear that you put some thought and effort into selecting something relevant and meaningful. Avoid sending gift cards or flowers unless you absolutely know it would be the perfect gift for that person. Gift cards and even flowers are impersonal and easily forgotten. Don't send food unless you know what they like. Send gifts that are tangible and that might live on their desks or that they might actually wear. Here's a list of some gifts that I recently gave to a few colleagues who spoke at one of my Heroic Public Speaking events. I mentioned a few of these folks in Chapter 12, in the discussion of rehearsals and wardrobe.

- Scott Stratten: Because Scott has a wild and long beard and a great sense of humor, I gave him a nice set of beard oils that have funny names like Lumberjack, Mechanic, Carpenter, Gentleman, and Bearded Barber.

- Bob Burg: I was inspired to pick this because Bob is emotional and sensitive and I wanted him to know that I like his work. I had a mug emblazoned with an inspirational quote that he wrote, YOUR TRUE WORTH IS DETERMINED BY

HOW MUCH MORE YOU GIVE IN VALUE THAN YOU TAKE IN PAYMENT.

- Barry Moltz: Because Barry had just returned from a life-changing trip to India, and because his business is about getting unstuck in your life or career, I gave him a statue of the Hindu deity Ganesha, the remover of obstacles.

- Chris Brogan: I chose food for Chris because I know how much he loves this stuff — Teddie Super Chunky Old Fashioned All Natural Peanut Butter and Smucker's Sugar Free Strawberry Preserves and a spoon.

- John Jantsch: In this instance, I chose beer from Boulevard Brewing Company because John has a personal connection with this company and loves microbrews. I also knew he'd be at the event long enough to enjoy the beer. To complement the gift, I gave him an R.E.I. bottle opener keychain because he's an outdoorsy kind of guy and might keep it with him.

The third phase is of course your balanced analysis and take-aways for your ongoing work. Most people care deeply about their work, and some, like me, are rarely ever satisfied with it. It is typically easier to obsess about the missed moments than to relish what worked and focus on what to do next time to improve the performance.

- The next day or two after the performance, make a list of what worked and what needs to be improved. This way you can continue to hone and improve the performance. This applies to all performance situations. For example, if you're in the job interview process, after each interview, make a similar "what worked and what needs to be improved" list and start rehearsing to produce the improvements. Avoid the mindset of *good* and *bad,* which colors your work with negativity. I like the Plus/Delta system of analysis that uses two columns — what is working that you want to continue (Plus), and what is not working that you want to change (Delta).

- If a video is available of your performance, don't review it until you've made some initial notes based on your experience of the performance. Then compare your notes to your analysis of the video. It can be helpful to do this review with a friend or advisor — particularly if you're new to watching tape of yourself, which can be disorienting and even disconcerting. All these notes go into your preparation and the next rehearsal.

OH, AND DID YOU FORGET ABOUT THAT STANDING OVATION?

I appreciate that you're still with me at this point in the book. I truly believe that, if you've made that kind of commitment, you deserve a standing ovation for every big presentation you make. A standing O will leave the entire room on an up note, which is good for you and your attendees. Everyone shares in the success.

So here's the idea: Have everyone in your audience stand up at the end of your presentation, just before you do your close. Seriously. Yes, I know I'm being a little cheeky in the simplicity of the advice. But it works brilliantly. Is it manufactured? You bet. But so is all show biz, from the pre-K "graduation" ceremony to a green-screened special effects blockbuster. You can find different reasons to do this — maybe an interactive game or other audience interaction technique, or simply to stretch their legs. But the truth is, I do it all the time and no one has called foul or sent it up to the league office for review. Besides, as an audience member yourself, I'm sure you agree with me that many times you want to stand but don't want to be the one who starts it. This loosens up that whole moment.

SPEED REVIEW

My five keys to a show-stealing performance will serve as your playbook for turning your rehearsed presentation into an actual live event that fulfills its potential. They are:

Pre-show ritual: Thoroughly prep the organizers and tech crew without alienating anyone; double-check your equipment and do your dry run and tech check; adopt a light warmup routine that keeps you loose and more at ease.

Developing stage awareness: Make yourself familiar with and adapt your performance to the physical limitations and realities of your performance space. Know how to seat your audience, deal with rickety risers, and tweak your blocking.

Owning the room: A staple for every experienced performer, owning the room involves projecting competence and a real command to give your audience confidence, using your physical presence to manage the live experience, and provoking the audience with manageable risks that pay off without going too far or seeming out of control.

Creating intimate moments: Emotional moments resonate and stick with your audience. You can make more emotional moments possible by the effective use of timing, feeling for and working your audience's energy level and your own, knowing how to smooth out and stay resilient through the inevitable duds and fails in a performance, and keeping in mind that your perceived performance is typically not as bad (or likely as good) as you may believe.

Managing the post-show cycle: Deftly handle this phase by first thanking the tech folks and mingling with the audience, then decompressing with peers or colleagues over a light meal; following up with personalized gifts and notes for organizers and other speakers who have been part of your event at your request, and all the others who helped you. Finally, after riding the initial wave of emotion, start your analysis of what worked and what you want to change.

Epilogue

All's Well That Ends Well

ANYONE CAN START SOMETHING. Only a few finish. You, my friend, are a finisher. And that is something that should make you proud. Together, we set out to demystify and learn everyday performance principles and techniques you can use to overcome your fears, silence your critics, find your voice, and become a confident performer. I took you inside the presentation process to show you where big ideas start and how they can come alive through your performance to change the world. I've left you with a nothing-like-it-in-the-world toolbox of how-tos and what-to-dos on speaking and public performance that you can grab whenever and however needed.

You've also encountered a lot of stories. I told you about how I left acting and used my training to land a job for which I wasn't technically qualified — but still turned out to be a great fit for my talents. You learned about my student Lori who found her voice after I took away her note cards. I told you about an astronaut who kept saying *yes, and* ... despite his fears and saved our ability to learn about deep space. I recounted how Olympic legend Herb Brooks used some serious role-playing to galvanize a historic performance from the 1980 U.S. men's ice hockey team. You met my student Brian Wolfinger, who found that my method saved the day when he didn't have his presentation slides. I gave you examples of how prominent CEOs, such as Tim Cook, grow by playing different roles — all of which are authentic.

But there's an important story missing — *yours*. Now you know that in order to take the stage in high-stakes situations that offer professional advancement and personal fulfillment you do not need to be an entertainer but a *performer*. And you know that role-playing works for CEOs and for presidents. In short, are you still waiting to find out what *your* story might become?

Have you asked yourself how you're going to leverage your strengths through public speaking and performing to experience more of what life has to offer? If so, here's how you can set off on a heroic journey and live the narrative that is the next and most fulfilling stage of your life. You start where all the good stories start: in Act One, with the given circumstances of where your life is now.

Maybe it's one o'clock in the morning and you're finishing up emails from a boss who drives you crazy and finds a way to avoid every conversation about the promotion you deserve. In six hours, you'll be getting dressed to do it all over again. You used to love your profession. Now, you're not so sure. What about your interest in graduate school? You've put it off for years.

Or you've gone through a bruising divorce from a spouse who kept you playing small and left you with emotional bruises too many times. You're not feeling great, but if you're going to make ends meet for you and your daughter, you're going to need a new job.

You're back at a favorite local café, having the same old conversation with a business buddy about how you'd like to start your own business — and you can see your friend can barely stay awake through the conversation. You ask yourself, do I have what it takes?

Maybe you're a nonprofit executive gone a little stale but you still have your sense of public service and there's a city council seat opening up in your community, where you are well known. As you go out for your morning jog, you can't stop thinking about how much you'd like to go for it. But you're not sure what your employer will say — and do you have the funds?

It's been years of dating here and there. It's been a long time since you've been in a great relationship. You've scraped out the dregs of the dating sites. You know your heart is open for love but you're beginning to wonder if it'll ever happen.

You're an IT executive with a dream of becoming CIO at a great *Fortune* 500 company. You'll have to raise your profile at more industry events and should be willing to relocate your family. Will your spouse go for that? She hasn't in the past. The other day, your boss offered you the chance to take his place on a panel at a regional conference. What could you do with the opportunity?

You're a writer with an idea for a book about the economy in Southeast Asia and you want to sell the proposal, go into publishers with a killer pitch, get a book contract, and travel for three months. But your significant other doesn't want you to go away, even for a short time.

What are your own hopes and dreams that you'll put on hold for another weekend? Which ones do you find a little too painful to examine? What are the dreams you want to take out into the world and make happen? How much money will you need? What kind of new career? What will your personal life look like? What kind of business will you run? What is the state of your dreams today? What are the consequences of not taking action?

Write down the real story based on the true given circumstances of your life in Act One.

Then move into Act Two, where you face formidable obstacles, both personal and professional, and wonder how you're going to surmount them. Welcome to the conflict in your life. Experience the tension of seeing and facing your challenges.

What is standing in your way? Is there a gap between your goals and your funds? Do you need a graduate degree but are terrified of leaving your career track? Can you dedicate the time away from your family to gun for the C-level job you want? Do you fear you're too old or too jaded for love? Are you torn between raising your kids and stepping up to a manager's job? Does a controlling relationship hold you back?

Be honest. Write down the toughest obstacles to your dream. And be prepared because Act Two is where you'll grapple with the performer's paradox. Remember? This is the common conundrum where your ambition to become a performer adds to your anxiety and fear because, like most of us, you have your fears activated by the specter-like possibility of being laughed at or rejected. So your ambition for good things for yourself can increase your resistance to achieving your goal. This is where knowledge is power: you ask yourself what you can achieve from what you learned in this book and how it will break the grip of the performer's paradox.

Now you can ask yourself: What are the things you're going to have to overcome? How will you lead the charge? What does the inner and outer struggle or challenge look like and what roles are you going to play to win the day?

Write down your Act Two. Your demons. The fears you want to do away with once and for all. The ways you'll take action.

On to your Act Three. Tension is rising but so is the hope that you can achieve transformation and find a resolution. Here is where you want to make your next remarkable performance. Here is where you identify and ultimately experience the rewards of a battle well fought and won. It's time to silence the critics.

You nail the interview you feared. You give the fund-raising speech and raise the bucks. You kick out the controlling lover and write your book proposal. You steal the show at an industry conference. You agree to one last blind date, find that he's a beautiful man, inside and out, and call him the next day. You're going to steal the show when you see him next. One speech, one performance won't be enough. But it'll potentially be more than you've done in a very long time to reach out and grab your dreams and never let go.

This is your Act Three. Write it down. Finish the story. Raise the stakes. Make what you're doing matter.

I want to hear about your stories and see if I can help along the way. Write to me at questions@michaelport.com and share your story. I want to know where you're going, what you must overcome, and how you're going to achieve rewards, blessings, and accomplishments using the techniques, protocols, and methodologies I've revealed in this book. And when you have wins along the way, I want to hear about those too.

The Cheat Sheet

*The 50 Public Speaking Tips You
Can't Afford to Ignore If You Want to
Wow Your Audience and
Win Praise and Plaudits Every Time*

USE THESE FIFTY TIPS TO REFRESH YOUR MEMORY when you're preparing for a presentation. However, if you haven't yet read the book but you're about to read these tips, please know that *Steal the Show* is not just about public speaking. Not everyone needs to be on a stage, wants to be on a stage, or will ever be on a stage. *People from all walks of life need help in everyday performance situations:* asking for a raise, nailing an interview, closing a deal, or leading a team meeting.

My suggestion is that no matter what kind of major presentation—job interview, sales pitch, industry conference—you're preparing for, take a few moments to review the items below as your final checklist to ensure that you're ready to steal the show.

1. **You DON'T have to tell them what you're going to tell them.** You've heard the old adage "Tell them what you're going to tell them; tell them; then tell them what you told them." It makes perfect sense and is perfectly appropriate

in some situations and can even be helpful. However, not all speeches need to open with a "here's what we're going to do today." In fact, sometimes taking the audience on a journey that they don't expect can be exciting. If the speech is good, you don't need to tell them what you're going to do. When you go to see a movie it rarely starts with the cast telling you what's going to happen for the next ninety minutes and that everyone dies in the end. And I am sure you've seen a movie trailer that has ruined the movie for you.

2. **Cut, cut, cut!** I often see (and you often see) extraneous detail added into stories and speeches that disrupts the flow. Cut to the meat. Cut to the chase. Include specifics at critical parts of the story. You don't need to pad out your speech to make an impact. Instead, you need to *focus* – with intention – on what's important. Your audience needs a lot less information to get to the "Aha!" moment than you might think.

3. **An entire story is designed to serve the end.** Whatever precedes the punch line must serve the payoff. Do I need to know what color socks you're wearing? Or how long it took you to get here today?

4. **The speech starts with your bio, before you walk on-stage.** That means that your introduction (known as your bio in the trade) should be powerful and impressive. Don't worry about sounding too proud of yourself: you can immediately disarm the audience with something sincere and self-effacing in the opening of your speech.

5. **Establish right away that you know what the world looks like for them – and what it could look like.** Vividly paint the picture. All world-saving performances are transformational experiences for the audience. Start out by showing "Here's what you've got today," and "Here's how it could

be." This builds immediate rapport and hooks the audience's interest. You know them. You understand them. You've got their backs . . . and you've got a better way.

6. **Reward your audience for participating or contributing in some way.** Now, you don't need to throw treats into the mouths of audience members to get their attention. But they are sentient and intelligent living beings who need simple acknowledgment if you want them to interact and contribute. Imagine being asked to participate in something – whether it's holding a door open for a friend or running a major project – and not even getting a nod of thanks in return.

7. **Use open hands with your palms up instead of your finger for pointing.** Sometimes the pointed finger looks like a gun. It's also a rude gesture in some cultures. Instead, extend your hand with the palm up as if offering up alms. It's more gracious, more inclusive, and more giving.

8. **People say *yes* when we've affected them intellectually, emotionally, or physically.** Can you include those three elements in your presentation? Can you give them intellectual gristle to chew on? Can you make them gasp or cry or laugh with an emotional connection? Can you get them physically engaged (you can tell by the way they're sitting) with your ideas and message? If not, it's probably because you're reading this cheat sheet before you've read the book.

9. **Outline your content and then unpack it.** If you're teaching content (which is distinct from a message-type speech), outline your material first, then go back and unpack it. This isn't the same as "tell them what you're going to tell them." It's a learning plan for what's coming next. It serves as both a high-level overview before you get granular and a teaser for the exciting content still to come.

10. **Use props.** What can you show or demonstrate or depict with objects rather than words? Can you stimulate your audience visually as well as auditorily? *Props aid recall:* If you want to be remembered, you can be visually arresting (without dying your hair) by using props to drive your points home. Most speakers don't do this. That's just one of the reasons why you should.

11. **Use contrast and extremes to create excitement and keep attention.** Contrast can be emotional, physical, and structural. This basic story-arc technique is integral to every great play, every great film, and every great piece of music. Consider your performance like a roller-coaster ride. Can you take me to the edge of a cliff before artfully lowering me, with love and care, to a safe place? Can you make the highs higher and the lows lower?

12. **Keep moving forward. Never let your energy drop.** You're on stage to take your audience to their final destination. Keep your foot on the gas pedal. You'll have uphill moments when your speed slows but the power and intensity increase. You can be both calm and energetic simultaneously.

13. **Audiences like to think that events on the stage are happening spontaneously.** They like to be surprised. The great actor does this brilliantly. You, as a speaker, need to do this as well. The best way to be effortlessly spontaneous is to rehearse to the point of mastery. How often do you have to stop and think about "spontaneously" adjusting your shoelaces? Never. When you know your material, you can deliver it like it's the first time *every time* you perform it.

14. **Stand and land.** Let your punch lines, point lines, and purpose lines *land*. That means you don't move while you're de-

livering them. You remain physically rooted to the spot so that your body reinforces the gravity of your words.

15. **You can move and talk at the same time.** People do it all the time in real life. The idea that you can't walk and talk at the same time is ridiculous. But don't sway, and don't move when you're landing your most important points (see number 14 above, Stand and land).

16. **Don't say, "I'm glad to be here."** *Show* them that you're glad to be there instead. Your audience should see it in your actions and hear it in your words. Besides, what's the alternative? That you're *not* glad to be there?

17. **Don't tell them you're going to tell a story.** Just tell the story.

18. **Be conscientious about connecting the dots or you'll lose your audience.** If you're presenting a series of interconnected concepts or stories or characters, make it as simple as possible to understand. Remember: even though you know your story inside out, your audience is hearing it for the first time.

19. **Give them time.** If you like to encourage note-taking during your performance, make sure you give people enough time to write down what you want them to write down. Spell things out if necessary. You'll lose your audience very quickly if they've got their heads stuck in their notebooks or laptops.

20. **Never apologize for the amount of time you don't have.** The minute you apologize for what they're not getting, your audience will start to feel that they're missing out on something. They should feel that the amount of time you have is the perfect amount of time. You can blow their minds in just

a few minutes. Look at all those great TED talks for inspiration.

21. **Let them go early.** Audiences always like to be let out a few minutes early – even if they love your performance. There are no prizes for endurance in performance. Let them leave a few minutes ahead of schedule; they'll thank you for it.

22. **Enlist the self-proclaimed experts in the room.** There's often somebody in the audience who knows more than you – or thinks they do. Get them on your side. Talk them up. Kill them with lavish praise. It'll help knock the chips off their shoulders and get them to support you and your message.

23. **Embellishment is positively OK.** You'll paint a more vivid picture with brighter colors. It's a performance, a show. Be honest, but embellish for the sake of your performance. You can combine multiple stories into one story if it produces a better result. Go for what is most dramatic and effective to get your message across.

24. **Remember that they don't know what you know.** It's the first time they've heard your info. Don't assume prior knowledge. It can only help your message if you're comprehensive and to the point.

25. **Don't use acronyms.** Or, if you do, explain them the first time around. Take the time to make them clear.

26. **Show them what the world will look like if they *don't* change.** Make it clear that if they don't follow your advice, or come with you on your journey, their world will probably remain the same as – if not get considerably worse than – it is today.

27. **Study standup comedy.** Watch standup comedians for their approach. Watch their setup, delivery, and payoff. See how they own the stage. Standup comedians can even turn a water bottle into a tool for creating magic moments.

28. **Be careful using idioms.** Across cultures — even cultures that share a language — there are big idiomatic differences that can turn your message opaque for an audience that doesn't "get it." If you're an American talking to a British audience about bangs, bleachers, boondoggles, or fanny-packs, you've likely lost them already.

29. **Don't make jokes about difficult topics.** Stay away from jokes that are awkward, insensitive, or otherwise confrontational. If you want to make yourself the butt of your jokes, that kind of self-deprecating humor can work very well. This doesn't mean you can't lighten up the mood when talking about difficult subjects, but that's different than poking fun or making jokes at other people's expense.

30. **If you tell them you care about something, you also need to tell them why.** It's not good enough to say, "I'm a strong proponent of women's rights." You've got to hook them in with your reasons. Your *why* is what makes your beliefs more powerful and your case stronger.

31. ***Boom, boom, BANG.*** The rule of three is one of the most important performance techniques you can use to grab attention and make people laugh. It's powerful, it's potent, and it packs a punch. (See what I did there?)

32. **Understand stage blocking.** You need to remain physically open so everyone in the room can see you at all times. That means you don't hide or turn to face anybody other than your audience . . . unless for dramatic effect.

33. **Deliver big moments center stage (usually).** Centering yourself physically on the stage is the same as bolding and centering a headline in a newspaper. It says: "This is important — pay attention!" When you designate center stage as the pivotal place for your performance, you can more effectively use the rest of the stage to support your main message. There are always exceptions to this concept, so be sure your blocking works before the big day.

34. **That said, don't head straight for center stage.** When getting onstage for the first time, avoid making a beeline directly to the center before starting your speech. It looks stiff and clunky.

35. **Learn how to rehearse.** Rehearsal is the absolute key to performance. It's not just repetition, but training. If you have to stop a rehearsal, start back up at the exact same emotional, physical, and energetic state. Otherwise, you'll lose the through-line and arc of the speech.

36. **When you land a joke, bask in it.** If public speaking is notoriously difficult, making people laugh when you're performing is devilishly tough. So, when you nail a joke, be sure to bask in the moment.

37. **Voice and speech training are not something you master in an hour.** It takes some time. I studied voice and speech daily for three years at NYU's Graduate Acting Program, and I'm still learning. Voice and speech training can make you sound more substantial so people will pay attention to you. It can also help you manage your nerves.

38. **Don't push.** Pushing is a theater term for overacting. When you push, you can't show emotion. When you push, the work feels false and self-absorbed. It's insincere. Insincerity is the enemy of truth. Truth is integral to performance.

39. **Just because you're feeling it, they might not be.** Major emotion for you as the speaker doesn't always translate to major emotion for your audience. It's only in rehearsal and practice that you find out what works and what doesn't. You might be moved to tears while your audience is bored to tears. Big difference.

40. **Get everything in before the audience claps.** Then, get off the stage quickly. Don't let them see you doing housekeeping or making routine announcements. It breaks the theatrical experience. You're the performer. They're not interested in watching you collect questionnaires from the audience.

41. **You can also stay onstage at the end if you invite them to join you there.** That way you're hosting the party. You don't want them grabbing you in the restroom: nothing dissipates magic like a damp handshake in the gent's.

42. **Anyone can make a sexy sizzle reel.** (If you're on the professional speaker track.) Meeting planners want to know you can hold the stage for an extended period of time. Make sure you can show them video of five to fifteen minutes of continuous performance where you deliver a strong message and truly engage the audience. No speaker gets hired just because he has a good video editor.

43. **Get right to it!** Most speakers waste time on too much exposition and preparation and the audience starts thinking, *Let's go already!* Instead, hit the accelerator hard and launch straight on. Let them know what they're in for by what they experience from you in the first thirty seconds.

44. **Stop using the storyteller voice.** It's false. Tell a story to ten thousand people the same way you'd tell the story to your best friend. Don't use some dramatic made-up voice. Study

your favorite speakers. They make you feel like it's just you and them in the room.

45. **Reduce.** You have no time for self-indulgence. You must be clinical and surgical with your material and your message. Don't use overly obfuscating verbiage when you can say things simply. We get attached to bits that really don't further the story or resonate with the audience, perhaps because they're funny or easy for us or have a special meaning to us. But it's not about us. It's never about us. It's about *them*.

46. **You don't have to slow down.** Most speech teachers tell you to slow down. Sometimes that makes sense. But if you're worried about speaking too quickly, you're focused on the wrong thing. Instead of slowing down, focus on *pausing*. Speakers who speak too slowly have a soporific effect. I speak quickly. But I pause at the right places. That creates rhythm. I slow down when it serves the speech to slow down. Audiences can easily absorb the important points if you give them pause time.

47. **If you have to explain a joke, it's just not funny.** No joke gets funnier with explanation. Choose a better joke or let it go altogether.

48. **Never turn your back to the audience unless it's intentional to make a point or convey an emotion.** When you need to move upstage (that's toward the back of the stage, away from the audience), walk backwards if possible. Try not to turn your back.

49. **Never yell at your audience.** This shouldn't need saying, but we sometimes let our standards slip when we're not in performance mode. You're *always* performing when you're in front of a group of people. If you need to get everybody's attention after a coffee break, for instance, simply raise your

hand and stand silently. People will get it and follow. That's powerful.

50. **If you think you're going to rise to the occasion, don't bet on it.** Under pressure, you don't rise to the occasion; you fall back on your training. If you think you're going to somehow be inspired to come up with the right material during the speech without hours of preparation, think again.

Most rules are made to be broken. But to break the rules of performance, you need to know what the rules are. You need to know why they exist and exactly why you're breaking them. When you break the rules with a real purpose, you can produce a better and more effective result.

You must be prepared if you want to make life-saving, world-changing speeches. That's what *Steal the Show* can do for you: make you a much, much better public speaker and performer in all aspects of life.

A performance can be about wowing an audience, but it can also be about simply connecting with one person. Most importantly, you don't have to be an entertainer to be a performer. And you don't have to think of yourself as a performer today to use what I teach in *Steal the Show* tomorrow.

Acknowledgments

GEORGE ORWELL SAID, "Writing a book is a horrible, exhausting struggle, like a long bout with some painful illness. One would never undertake such a thing if one were not driven on by some demon whom one can neither resist nor understand." That just about sums it up. There is no way I could have made it through the bout without the people in my corner who have my back. This book, my work, and my happiness would not be possible without the contributions, guidance, teaching, and support of many others . . . including you.

Amy, I'm yours, forever, in life and work, and I'm a better man because of you. Herb, Stephen, and Rick, you three are the best writing partner, agent, and editor, respectively, that any author could hope for. Matthew, Jaimie, Dan, Cosmin, Francine, and Ana, just writing your names brings tears of gratitude to my eyes; none of this would be possible without you. Mom, Dad, Jake, and Pearl, your love and support is unflinching and lifts me up when I am down. Dad, your commitment to the truth along with your ethical standards serve as my personal compass for right and wrong. Alex, Neal, and Ben, since we can't make new old friends, I'm stuck with you three, and I love you for it. My fellow colleagues and authors, you challenge me to be better and work harder every day. Ron Van Lieu, the faculty, and my classmates at NYU's Graduate Acting Program, you taught me how to understand as well as express myself in service of an audience. My clients and students, it is you whom I proudly serve; your courage, commitment, and passion never cease to amaze me. To those who helped me select the title *Steal the Show,* thank you. You'll see your names in print in the backmatter of the e-book. Last, but certainly not least, my dear reader, every day I do my best for you and hope that it is good enough.

Notes

1. Find Your Voice

1. Branden, Nathaniel. *The Six Pillars of Self Esteem* (New York: Bantam Books, 1994).

2. Play the Right Role in Every Situation

1. Ibarra, Herminia, "The Paradox of Authenticity," *Harvard Business Review,* January 2015, https://hbr.org/2015/01/the-authenticity-paradox.

3. Crush Your Fears and Silence the Critics

1. Itskoff, Dave, "The Other Super Bowl Underdog," *New York Times,* January 30, 2014, http://www.nytimes.com/2014/01/31/arts/music/bruno-mars-says-hes-ready-for-his-big-stage.html.
2. Strecker, Erin, "Idina Menzel Defends New Year's Eve Performance," *Billboard,* January 2, 2015, http://www.billboard

.com/articles/news/6429348/idina-menzel-defends-new
-years-eve-performance.

4. Have a Clear Objective

Epigraph: Cannon, Dee, and Lyn Gardner, "Character Building
and What Makes a Truly Great Actor," *The Guardian,* May
9, 2009, http://www.theguardian.com/stage/2009/may/09/
character-building-great-actor.

1. Zander, B. (2008, February). Benjamin Zander: The
   transformative power of classical music [Video file]. Retrieved
   from http://www.ted.com/talks/benjamin_zander_on_music
   _and_passion?language=en.

5. Act "As if . . ."

1. Newmark, Thomas, "Cases in Visualization for Improved
   Athletic Performance," *Psychiatric Annals* 42, no. 10 (October
   2012): 385–387.
2. Cohen, Elizabeth, "Can You Imagine Cancer Away?" CNN.com,
   March 3, 2011, http://www.cnn.com/2011/HEALTH/03/03/
   ep.seidler.cancer.mind.body/.
3. Carny, Cuddy, and Yap, "Power Posing: Brief Nonverbal
   Displays Affect Neuroendocrine Levels and Risk Tolerance,"
   Psychological Science XX(X) 1–6, September 20, 2010, http://
   www.people.hbs.edu/acuddy/in%20press,%20carney,%20
   cuddy,%20&%20yap,%20psych%20science.pdf.

7. Say "Yes, and . . ."

1. "Google's Eric Schmidt to graduates: 'Find a way to say YES
   to things,'" UC Berkeley News Center, May 14, 2012, http://
   newscenter.berkeley.edu/2012/05/14/google-ceo-to-graduates
   -the-future-doesnt-just-happen/.

2. Hanson, Rick, "When Good Is Stronger Than Bad," http://www.rickhanson.net/teaching/tgc-public-summary/.
3. Rock, David, "SCARF: a brain-based model for collaborating with and influencing others," *NeuroLeadership Journal* 8, no. 1, 2008.
4. Ibid.

8. Be in the Moment

1. Berry, Cicely. *Voice and the Actor* (New York: Wiley, 1991).
2. Horowitz, Seth, "The Science and Art of Listening," *New York Times,* November 9, 2012, http://www.nytimes.com/2012/11/11/opinion/sunday/why-listening-is-so-much-more-than-hearing.html.
3. Wallace, Craig, "Quiet! Someone's Getting the Job!" *Backstage,* December 2, 2009, http://www.backstage.com/advice-for-actors/acting-teachers/quiet-someones-getting-the-job/.

9. Choose Early and Often

1. Rowling, J. K. *Harry Potter and the Chamber of Secrets* (New York: Arthur Levine Books/Scholastic, 1998).

11. How to Create and Tell Stories That Make 'Em Laugh or Cry

1. Cosper, Amy, "The Year of the Story," *Entrepreneur,* http://www.entrepreneur.com/article/239142.

14. How to Improvise Your Way into the Hearts and Minds of the Toughest Crowds

1. Bilton, Nick, "A Master of Improv, Writing Twitter's Script," *New York Times,* October 6, 2012, http://www.nytimes.com/2012/10/07/technology/dick-costolo-of-twitter-an-improv-master-writing-its-script.html?pagewanted=all&_r=0.

15. How to Get a Standing Ovation Every Time — Really

1. Rupani-Smith, Sylvia, "Actors' Pre- and Post-Show Rituals," *New York Times,* December 4, 2014, http://www.nytimes.com /video/t-magazine/100000003269702/actors-pre-and-post -show-rituals.html.
2. Sommer, Sarah, "10 Habits of Highly Successful Athletes," *Men's Journal,* http://www.mensjournal.com/expert-advice /10-habits-of-highly-successful-athletes-20131203/calvin -johnson#ixzz3R54PTxrw.

Index